ISBN 978-1-333-56870-2
PIBN 10520831

LESSONS

IN

PRACTICAL SCIENCE:

OR,

GENERAL KNOWLEDGE REGARDING THINGS IN DAILY USE.

PREPARED EXPRESSLY FOR

SCHOOLS AND ACADEMIES,

BY

THE AUTHOR OF THE NEPTUNE OUTWARD BOUND, THE NEPTUNE AFLOAT, &c.

Sister Francis de Sales Chase, resident the convent of the Visitation, Ottumwa, Io

NEW YORK:

P. O'SHEA, AGENT,

37 BARCLAY STREET.

1879.

147
R67

TO THE PAST AND PRESENT PUPILS OF THE

VISITATION ACADEMY, OTTUMWA, IOWA,

With whom I have passed so many pleasant years, I dedicate this

Volume, with the earnest desire that they may ever

advance in the knowledge of true wisdom.

Their sincere friend,

THE AUTHOR.

PREFACE.

THE WORK OF EDUCATION is a great one, in truth *the* greatest we have to accomplish "wisely and well," since it includes the culture of body, mind and heart.

A great writer has truly said : "How to live, how worthily to dispose of that one life, which is all wherewith each of us has to face Eternity, is confessedly the gravest problem a sane man can be called to solve."

This is the work of the Educator in training the youth committed to his charge. To assist him, books have so multiplied in the primary as well as higher branches, that pouring forth from busy brains and printing presses as if by magic, they would seem to have exhausted the subjects of which they treat. And yet, with all this multiplicity, there still seemed to be a void—an omission, viz.: works of a more practical nature, treating of objects in constant use, of which children as well as older persons were ignorant. An attempt has been made to supply this deficiency in the present volume. Its limits excluded many subjects of which we would gladly have treated. The great difficulty was to select from so many necessary and useful objects, the comparatively few treated here.

The continual improvements in the works of man, as well as fresh discoveries in nature, will always make such an attempt as this more or less incomplete. A few links only are here given from the great chain of knowledge, which like the circle, the ancient symbol of eternity, has neither beginning or end. Although mainly intended for the class-room, we trust this work will also find a welcome in the family circle.

ALPHABETICAL INDEX.

CONTENTS.

SECTION I.

CHAPTER I.

GENERAL IMPROVEMENTS.

SECTION II.

CHAPTER I.

GLASS.—ITS EARLY HISTORY.

CHAPTER II.

METHOD OF MAKING GLASS.

CHAPTER III.

PLATE-GLASS.

CHAPTER IV.

GLASS ORNAMENTS.

SECTION III.

CHAPTER I.

POTTERY AND PORCELAIN.

Pottery.

CHAPTER II.

ETRUSCAN WARE.

CHAPTER III.

VARIETIES IN POTTERY AND PORCELAIN.

CHAPTER IV.

METHOD OF MAKING POTTERY AND PORCELAIN.

SECTION IV.

CHAPTER I.

. PAPER.

SECTION V.

CHAPTER I.

PRINTING.

CHAPTER II.

MODERN METHOD OF PRINTING.

CHAPTER III.

PROCESS OF PRINTING EXPLAINED.

CHAPTER IV.

STEREOTYPE PRINTING.

SECTION VI.

CHAPTER I.

COTTON MANUFACTURERS.

CHAPTER II.

PROGRESS OF THE MANUFACTURE IN DIFFERENT COUNTRIES.

CHAPTER III.

METHOD OF MANUFACTURE.

CHAPTER IV.

GREATER IMPROVEMENTS.

CHAPTER V.

CALICO PRINTING.

SECTION VII.

SECTION VIII.

CHAPTER III.

GUTTA–PERCHA.

SECTION X.

CHAPTER I.

CLOCKS AND WATCHES.

CHAPTER II.

AMERICAN CLOCKS.

SECTION XII.

CUTLERY.

CHAPTER I.

CUTLERY IN GENERAL.

CHAPTER II.

KNIVES AND FORKS.

CHAPTER III.

OTHER ARTICLES OF CUTLERY.

CHAPTER IV.

CUTLERY IN THE UNITED STATES.

SECTION XIII.

PINS AND NEEDLES

CHAPTER I.

PINS.

CHAPTER II.

NEEDLES.

SECTION XIV.

MONEY.

CHAPTER I.

COINS.

CHAPTER II.

PAPER MONEY.

SECTION XV.

TELEGRAPHY.

CHAPTER I.

THE ELECTRIC TELEGRAPH.

CHAPTER III

SUB–MARINE TELEGRAPH.

CHAPTER IV.
THE TELEPHONE.

CHAPTER V.
THE PHONOGRAPH.

SECTION XVI.

SUGAR.

CHAPTER I.

SUGAR—CANE.

CHAPTER II.

MAPLE.—SORGHUM.—BEET SUGAR.

SECTION XVII.

TEA.

CHAPTER I.

TEA.

B

SECTION XVIII.
COAL.
CHAPTER I.

FORMATION OF COAL.

CHAPTER II.

USEFUL SUBSTANCES OBTAINED FROM COAL.

CHAPTER III.

GAS.

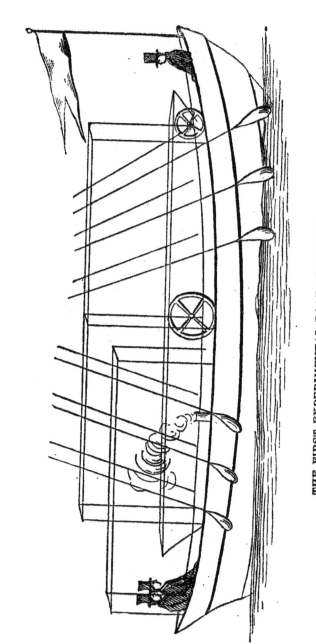

THE FIRST EXPERIMENTAL BOAT OF JOHN FITCH,

LESSONS IN
PRACTICAL SCIENCE.

SECTION I.

CHAPTER I.

GENERAL IMPROVEMENTS.

What are we to learn in this book?

About many things that we see every day, but of which we know very little.

What are some of them?

Paper, printing, glass, pottery, porcelain, plated-ware, etc.

As we look around us, how many different works do we find?

Two: those of Nature and Art.

How do they differ?

The works of Nature are made by God, those of Art by man.

Give examples of each.

Animals, plants, oceans, mountains, etc., are works of nature. Railroads, steamers, buildings and their furniture, are works of Art.

Can man make any of the works of God?

No; not a single one, even so much as a little grain of sand.

What other great difference do we find between works of Nature and Art?

The former are always complete and perfect, while the latter are far from being so.

What does this teach us?

That Almighty God is very great and powerful, but man can do little or nothing.

How may works of art be divided?

Into the useful and ornamental.

Explain the difference between them.

The useful include such as are necessary for us, the ornamental are merely for giving pleasure.

Will you give examples of both?

Glass, paper, machines, etc., are among useful things ; music, painting, sculpture, etc., are ornamental.

Have any improvements ever been made in works of art?

Yes, a great many are made every day, but the works of God can never be changed or improved, being always perfect from the very beginning.

Did the people who lived hundreds of years ago have as many useful things as we now possess?

No, indeed ; they had only a few of the very simplest.

Why is this so?

Because every year new discoveries or inventions are made, which gradually lead to others, so that we are now supplied with every thing necessary for our use, comfort and pleasure.

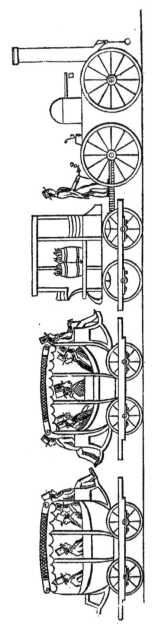

The First Passenger Train used on the Mohawk Valley R. R.

What are some of the things in which improvements have been made?

In farming, modes of travelling, manufacturing goods and many others.

Mention some of the changes that have taken place in farming.

Before the invention of machines, farmers did their work by hand, or with the aid of a few simple instruments.

How is the labor now performed?

The grain is planted, hoed, mowed, reaped, then threshed, winnowed, and even measured and placed in bags for the market, all by machines.

What advantage in this?

Much labor is saved, and more work can be done in the same time.

Give some example.

Threshing grain used to be done by hand with a flail, and one man could only thresh out from 10 to 15 bushels per day.

How can such work now be done?

The largest machines turn out from 600 to 1,200 bushels in the same time.

Will you relate an instance showing the power of the American Reaping Machines?

In the summer of 1855 a grand prize was offered in France for the best reaping machine that could be exhibited.

Who were allowed to contend for the prize?

Persons from all parts of the world.

Did any make the attempt ?

Yes.   At the first trial three machines appeared.
One from Algiers, another from England and the
third from America.

Where is Algiers ?

It is separated from France by the St. of Gibraltar.

*Where did this trial of skill with the machines take
place ?*

About 40 miles from Paris.

How much did each machine reap ?

About an acre ; reaping as well as cutting.

What was the result of the contest ?

The American finished the work in 22 minutes, the
English in 66, and the one from Algiers in 72.

Were any other attempts made ?

Yes.   And in all of them the Americans won the
prize.

Is the work as well done by machinery as by hand ?

Yes ; far better.

Are all machines perfect that are now in use ?

By no means.   Nothing made by man can ever be
so.   This is only true of the works of God.

*What implements did farmers use in the early history
of this country ?*

A plough, spade, clumsy wooden fork and sometimes a harrow.

Were all these well made ?

No ; very far from it.   The plough was entirely of
wood except a small point of iron at the end fastened
with straps of rawhide.

A PLOUGH.

How was it worked?

It was drawn by oxen yoked to the plough by the horns, then one strong man pressed it into the ground, another held and guided it, while a third drove.

How are the best ploughs now made?

They are made of cast iron and worked by steam.

Were there many ploughs in this country at that time?

No, very few. In 1637 only 37 in the colony of Mass. Bay, and for 12 years after the landing of the Pilgrims the farmers about Boston had none at all.

How did they break up the soil for planting seeds?

With rude kinds of hoes or mattocks, and when ploughs were introduced, for a long time there were so few, it was the custom for those who owned them to go round from house to house and do the ploughing for the rest of the farmers.

Why were not improvements made more rapidly?

The early settlers of our country seemed to think it necessary to follow the customs of their fathers.

If a person proposed any thing new, what did the people think?

They looked upon him as very foolish, or half crazy.

What were some of their strange ideas?

A young farmer thought he must plant as many acres of corn and wheat as his father had done, and on the same land.

At what time?

When the moon was old, that is when it rose very late in the evening; then they felt certain of a good crop.

Upon what does a good crop really depend?

It depends upon the proper soil and fine weather.

Did the farmers then cultivate the soil?

Very little, and rather than take the trouble to carry the rich earth from their barn-yards to the corn and wheat fields, they preferred to move the barn away.

Did they have a " Rotation of Crops?"

No ; they knew nothing of it.

What is meant by a " Rotation of Crops?"

Planting different grains in the same field year after year.

Give an example.

If wheat is planted this year in a field, corn can be sowed the next season on the same land, and the third spring, rye, then oats or hemp, and so on through all the grains.

After that, what should be done?

Begin again with wheat and go through them as before.

Why is this the best plan?

Because each grain takes something from the soil that the others do not, which is necessary for its growth and nourishment.

Then if the crops are changed every year in the same field, what will happen?

There will be a chance for that part of the earth to form again in the ground, which was taken this season by the corn or wheat, and after a few years the soil will be ready for it again.

As the farmers did not adopt this plan of a Rotation of Crops, what was the consequence?

The land was soon worn out, and of course became almost worthless.

———

What changes have taken place in modes of traveling?

Steamships and cars are now used instead of sail-boats and wagons.

What is the principal cause of this change?

The discovery of the use of steam, and its application to many purposes.

To whom are we indebted for this great discovery?

We are indebted to James Watts, a Scotchman.

When did he live and what do you know of him?

He was born in 1736; died in 1819. From his boyhood he spent much time in studying out every thing curious or wonderful that came in his way.

How did he find out the power of steam?

It is said he learned this by noticing that steam would raise the lid of his mother's teakettle whenever the water boiled.

What happened one day?

He was watching the kettle as usual, and as he could not hold down the lid with a stick he thought he would tie it with a strong cord and close up the spout.

What was the result of his experiment?

The steam had no chance to escape, and so burst the kettle, causing it to fly into a thousand pieces.

Is steam used for any thing else except boats and cars?

Yes; it is applied to many machines for manufacturing goods, heating buildings and for various other purposes.

What advantage is gained by this improvement in modes of travelling?

We can go much more quickly and pleasantly from place to place than formerly.

Give some examples.

Before the use of steam in this way, in 1805, it required 90 days, or about three months, for 10 persons to travel from Conn. to Ohio, the distance being 600 miles; but now 360 passengers can go from Conn. to Iowa, which is 1,300 miles, in 3 days.

Can you give another example?

The distance from New York to San Francisco is 3,756 miles. Formerly travellers were six months in making the trip; now it can be accomplished in seven days.

Have the improvements in manufacturing goods been as great as in farming and travelling?

Certainly, and perhaps even greater.

Before the invention of so many different machines, how was woollen cloth prepared for use?

The wool was carded, spun and woven by hand, then sent to a mill to be fulled, dyed and dressed.

When was the work commenced in this country ?

It began as a regular business in 1765, in New York, where a society was formed, the members pledging themselves not to wear clothes made in foreign countries.

What law was passed to increase the quantity of wool in the United States ?

A law was passed forbidding farmers to kill their sheep, or to purchase and even eat any mutton.

Did they then understand dressing and dyeing cloth ?

Very imperfectly. They did not know how to "fix" the colors, that is, to keep them from fading.

What incident can you relate to prove this ?

When Daniel Webster, the great statesman, was a boy, he prepared to go away to school, and for the occasion had a new suit of home-spun blue. While on the way to school he was overtaken by a sudden shower, and all the color washed out of his new clothes.

What other great invention during the present century may be added to the others ?

That of the magnetic telegraph.

When and by whom was it first brought into use ?

Experiments have been made at various periods in foreign countries. But in the United States the honor of making it practically useful is due to Prof. Morse. He first made known the success of his experiment in 1832.

When was the first message sent in this country ?

In 1844, between Washington and Baltimore. In

1857 there were 22,000 miles of telegraphic line. It extended from Halifax to New Orleans, and thence to Dubuque, Iowa. This shows how rapid has been the spread of the great invention in 12 years.

Is it still progressing?

Yes; and so much, that there is hardly a town or village through which the telegraph wire does not pass.

SECTION II.

CHAPTER I.

GLASS.—EARLY HISTORY.—MATERIALS USED.

Is the manufacture of Glass a new art?

No ; it is very old.

What proof of this?

It must have been known to the ancients, as various articles made of glass are found among the ruins of their famous cities.

When and by whom was it first made?

This is not known. Many nations claim the honor, but there is no certain proof that it belongs to one more than another.

In what country can we trace it to the earliest date?

In Egypt ; glass beads are found there on the mummies, which are more than 3000 years old.

What are mummies?

The bodies of the ancient Egyptians that have been preserved for thousands of years.

How was this done?

It is not now known. The art of embalming dead bodies being lost. They are always found wrapped in cloths, in which different spices have been placed.

Are there any mummies now to be seen?

Yes; a great many in the tombs of the ancient Egyptians. Some have also been brought to this country for exhibition and to be placed in museums.

How do they look ?

The flesh is dried and wrinkled, so that a young girl of 20 would look like an old woman of 90 years. Yet the hair, teeth and all parts of the body are perfectly preserved.

Has glass been found anywhere else ?

Yes ; in the ruins of Nineveh glass bottles and vases were discovered.

How long ago was that ?

At least 4000 years, for Nineveh was founded more than 2000 B.C., when it became a great and powerful kingdom.

Does it still remain so ?

No. It has long since been utterly destroyed, so that even the place where it was situated is not certainly known.

Can you mention other cities where glass was also used ?

At Pompeii and Herculaneum.

Where are they ?

These were formerly famous cities at the foot of Mt. Vesuvius, in Italy. By an eruption of that volcano, they were so completely buried under the lava, nearly 2000 years ago, that they have only recently been discovered.

How did this happen?

Some workmen, who were digging a well, accidentally uncovered a portion of Pompèii.

What has since been done?

Other parts of the city have been laid open.

What are found there?

Many curious and beautiful things, all being just as
they were left by the people at the time of the eruption.

What have we learned by the discovery of these cities?

That the inhabitants were very wise and skilful,
and knew many things of which we supposed people
at that time were ignorant.

What are some of the curious articles found?

Many handsome urns, jars and vases, beautiful pictures, ornaments of gold, silver and precious stones.

What use did the people then make of glass?

They used it for windows, dishes and ornamental
objects, some of which are very beautiful.

How did they make it?

This is not known.

Was it used in other parts of Europe?

Yes ; the people of Italy carried the art of making it
into Gaul.

Where is Gaul?

It was the ancient name for France.

Why was it changed?

Because the Franks, a rude nation from Germany,
went there to settle, and having gained possession of
the country, gave their own name to it.

In what other country was glass made ?

In Bohemia, a division of Germany.

What was the quality of the glass made there ?

It was very fine ; indeed the best, and is still highly prized.

What is it called?

Bohemian glass.

When was glass introduced into England?

In 1439, and afterwards into America.

Has glass been found of much use?

Glass is very useful.

Mention some articles made of it.

It is used for windows, doors, and even houses, for table furniture, faces for clocks, watches, etc.

Are there any others ?

Yes ; a great many, as spectacles, microscopes, spy-glasses, telescopes, etc.

Is the same kind of glass used for all these things?

By no means. There is a great variety in the form, quality, color, etc.

Mention some of these differences.

Glass may be round or square, flat or curved, thick or thin, clear or opaque, colored or not, very plain or highly ornamented with figures raised or painted upon it, and of all grades from the poorest quality to the very best.

What is the cause of all these varieties?

It is owing to the materials used, as well as to the different ways in which the glass is manufactured.

What names have been given to the various kinds of glass?

Flint, Plate, Bohemian, Crystal, Enamel, Window, Bottle, and Opal; Flint being the best, and that for bottles the poorest.

What materials are used in making the finest kind of glass?

The very best quality of sand, refined potash, chalk, and manganese.

Of what is window glass composed?

It is formed of sand, chalk, soda, broken glass, arsenic, and manganese.

What has been lately used instead of soda?

Kryolite, a substance from which soda is readily made.

Where is it found?

At Ivigtut, in the S. E. part of Greenland.

Has it been found anywhere else?

It has not been discovered at any other place; but it is very abundant there, and over 3000 tons are taken every year for making hot cast porcelain, a kind of opaque glass.

For what is this porcelain used?

It is used for many things which were formerly made of glass; also for tiling floors.

Why is it preferred to glass?

Because it is much cheaper and more beautiful.

Where are the largest establishments for making this porcelain?

At Philadelphia.

CHAPTER II.

METHOD OF MAKING GLASS.

You said different materials were used for the various kinds of glass: does each one require a different process?

No; generally speaking the process is the same, except, of course, when peculiar forms are to be given to the articles made.

What is the first thing done by the workmen?

They select the materials to be used, carefully weighing them so there shall be the right quantity of each.

What is the next step?

These materials are then ground very fine, mixed together and sifted, so that the coarse, impure parts may not be used.

Is the whole mixture taken at once?

No; only about one-eighth, because it is necessary to melt it gradually and thoroughly.

MANUFACTURE OF GLASS.

When properly prepared in what is the mixture placed?

In about ten or twelve melting pots, which are heated to *white heat.*

What do you mean by white heat?

When iron or any other metal is heated very much, we say it is *red hot;* but when this heat is increased so as to look *white* instead of *red,* we call it *white heat.*

How long does the mixture remain in the melting-pots?

Until it has become thoroughly cooked.

How is this known?

The workmen take out a little of it ; if it is per-fectly clear when cooled, then it is ready to form into glass.

While the mixture is heating what takes place?

A scum rises to the top, caused by the impurities in the materials used ; this is of course removed until none appears.

Is the heat the same all the time?

No ; it is constantly increasing until it is made as great as possible.

Will the glass now look perfectly clear?

No ; there is a kind of gas formed which makes those bubbles we sometimes see in common glass if it is not removed.

How is this done?

By keeping the mixture at white heat for forty-eight hours after it is thoroughly melted.

2

What will happen then?

The bubbles disappear, and those substances that do not melt settle at the bottom.

Can the mixture now be formed into glass ?

Not yet ; for it is so hot as to be in a fluid state, that is, like water, and therefore must cool enough to be worked.

How great a quantity is usually prepared at once?

Enough to keep workmen employed night and day for at least four days ; each set of men is changed every six hours.

How is the glass blown?

The workman uses a pipe or blowing tube four or five feet long, a little larger at the mouth end than at the other, and takes as much of the mixture as is required ; if for window-glass, nine pounds are usually taken at once, there being about half a ton of the metal in each pot.

What is then done ?

The workman rolls the lump he has taken and allowed to cool, upon a polished cast-iron slab, called a *marver*, at the same time that he blows through the tube which causes the lump to swell. It is then heated in the furnace and again rolled and enlarged still more by blowing.

What shape does it now have?

The part nearest the tube becomes hollow, while the rest of the glass works towards the other end, where by rolling it forms into a cone.

What is this part called?

It is called the *bullion,* and when heated again the tube is allowed to rest on a support prepared for it, while the glass is blown into a globe.

Is the globe held still while blown?

No ; it is made to turn rapidly around all the while, which increases the size and gradually flattens it out.

Where is the glass the thickest?

At the *bullion point.*

Is any use made of this point?

Yes ; when the workman sees he has blown the globe sufficiently, he takes an iron rod called a *pontil,* on which there is a little melted glass and applies it to the bullion making it fast to the rod.

What is done at the other end?

At the same time the globe is separated from the blow-pipe by touching it with a piece of cold iron, leaving the globe upon the pontil.

What is left at the place where it was joined to the pipe?

A round hole; this is held by the pontil to the furnace until it is heated almost to melting, at the same time it is made to revolve very rapidly which causes the opening to enlarge by centrifugal force.

What is centrifugal force?

That which causes any thing to fly from the centre.

Can you give an example?

If you fasten a ball to a string and make it whirl round very rapidly, the centrifugal force will make it try to fly away; but there is another power, called *centripetal*, which is also drawing it to the centre.

Which is the greater of the two?

In this case they are exactly equal, so that the ball neither goes to nor from the centre, but in a circle.

Will you tell me if any thing else is affected in this way by these two motions?

Yes, many things; but the greatest of all are the planets that revolve around the sun.

What is the centre of their motion?

The Sun, which is all the time drawing these planets towards itself; but the other force called centrifugal, is also exerting its power, and, being just as great as the centripetal, the planets do not go either towards the sun or away from it, but in paths called orbits, which are more or less like a circle.

After holding the bullion to the furnace what takes place?

The opening having greatly increased in size, and the globe now being so nearly flat that the two opposite sides almost meet, the part nearest the fire seems to roll inside out.

How does the globe appear?

It has become a flat, circular piece of glass.

What is then done with it?

It is removed from the fire, and kept turning constantly until cooled.

Why is this necessary?

Because one part would cool sooner than another, becoming thick in some places and thin in others, the edges would warp or curl up, making the glass very imperfect.

What next takes place ?

After cooling sufficiently, the pontil is cracked off from the glass, and the circular sheet set on edge in the annealing oven with other sheets.

How long do they remain there ?

Usually one or two days.

Are these sheets perfectly cold ?

By no means ; only cool enough to keep the required shape.

What do you mean by annealing?

Simply placing the heated glass in a hot oven and allowing both to cool together.

Why is this necessary ?

Because if glass is not perfectly annealed, it will break very easily, or when cracked, fall to pieces.

Explain the reason ?

When hot glass is exposed to sudden cold, the outer part cools first, leaving the inside still partly melted, giving it no chance to expand as glass usually does when cooling, and which is necessary that the particles composing it may have their proper place, and the whole mass become tough and elastic.

Will you give an example of glass suddenly cooled ?

There is a toy called " Prince Rupert's Drops," made by dropping hot glass into cold water.

What effect is produced?

Most of the drops will burst—a few are formed into pear-shaped figures. If the least break takes place at the stem, they will fly open with a loud explosion.

What is done with the glass plates when taken from the annealing kiln?

They are removed to the warehouse and assorted; the purest and best sheets placed together; if any have too many defects they are cast aside.

How are the plates then cut?

By means of a diamond, into whatever shape is required. This is the kind of glass used for windows and such purposes.

How many of these plates are made at once?

If half a ton of the mixture is used in each pot, about one hundred tables can be made from eight such pots in three or four days.

What are some of the instruments used in handling the glass, while manufactured?

Besides the Pontil, already mentioned, there are spring-tongs, for taking up bits of melted glass, also a heavier pair called Pucellas, with broad, blunt blades, used to shape the article as it is rolled, very much as potters shape their clay vessels.

Can you mention any other?

A pair of shears is also used, by which the workman can clip off the top of a wine-glass or cup which is already shaped, while he twirls it around on the rod held in his left hand.

Are the edges perfectly even?

No; but they can be made so, by softening in the fire, then smoothing and polishing. A battle-door is also used to flatten glass when warm, by beating.

Do you know of any more instruments ?

A slender rod of iron, forked at one end, for taking articles not yet cool to the annealing oven to be tempered. The Marver is also very necessary.

What is that ?

A polished cast-iron slab, on which glass is rolled to make it perfectly round.

How long has colored window glass been used ?

As early as the 8th century we find churches supplied with it.

Was it also seen in private houses ?

Not for a long time ; even as late as the 12th century, private dwellings with glass windows were thought magnificent.

CHAPTER III.

PLATE-GLASS.

For what is plate-glass mostly used ?

For mirrors, and for windows in large and handsome buildings.

What are used in making it ?

The same materials as for crown-glass just described, except a greater quantity of soda is used, making the mixture more fluid and giving it a greenish or bluish tint. Greater care is also taken to have the materials pure, and free from all defects.

Why is this so necessary ?

Because in plate-glass, if there were defects, the light would be reflected or refracted irregularly, making the image formed on it imperfect.

Can you give some account of the process for making plate-glass ?

When the mixture is thoroughly melted it is either poured into red-hot cisterns or kept in the pots, and emptied from them upon casting tables.

What are casting tables ?

They are large metal tables, formerly made of bronze, but now of cast iron, because not so liable to crack.

How large are they ?

They vary in size. Those used at the Thames Glass Works in England are 20 ft. long, 11 broad and 7 inches thick.

How are the tables heated ?

By covering them with burning coals, which are afterwards taken off, and the surface of the metal made perfectly clean.

What is then done ?

The melted glass which has been allowed to cool a little is poured over these tables.

How is it prevented from running over the edges.

A ledge of iron passes all around the sides, being just the height required for the thickness of the glass.

What is done after pouring on the heated mixture ?

A copper cylinder or tube, about 3 ft. thick, rests on the edges, and being rolled back and forth, removes all the surplus glass.

Why is this necessary ?

Because the plate might then be thicker in some parts than others, but by this process it is made perfectly even throughout.

What is done with each plate when finished ?

It is taken to the annealing oven, and while the metal table is still hot, more melted glass is poured on, and other plates are made in the same way until all are complete.

How long are the plates kept in the oven ?

About five days : in France less time is required for annealing.

When properly annealed what is the next process ?

The plates are thoroughly examined so as to see how they can be cut to the best advantage in whatever shape is required.

How is the glass polished ?

Various methods are used. One is to place the plates on frames in beds of plaster-of-Paris ; by the working of machinery all the roughness is removed, and the glass becomes very smooth and bright.

FLINT-GLASS.

How does this differ from plate-glass ?

It differs in being made of much nicer materials. Still greater care is also taken to have it perfectly free from all impurities.

For what is flint-glass used ?

It is used for spectacles and optical instruments.

What are optical instruments ?

Opera glasses, microscopes, spy-glasses, telescopes, etc.

Why is flint-glass used in them ?

Because it is the best that is made, and as these instruments are intended for looking at objects that are so small or so far away that they cannot be seen by the naked eye, it is necessary the glass should be so clear that all the light may pass through it.

If these glasses are not well made, how will objects appear?

They will not be seen at all, or at least very indistinctly.

Are the melting pots used for flint-glass like those for crown and plate glass?

Not exactly. They are closed at the top, and have an opening through a short neck on the side.

Why are they made in this way?

To prevent the smoke from reaching the mixture, as it would discolor the glass.

Can you mention any other difference?

A greater degree of heat is used, so that the mixture is more quickly melted, and there is less danger of the iron from the pot acting upon it, which would make the glass worthless.

How are the articles shaped?

By blowing in moulds kept very hot.

Is there any other way?

Yes; by means of a die.

What is a die?

It is a piece of metal on which figures have been cut; from it impressions can be taken for coins, medals, etc., also for many articles made of glass.

How is flint-glass cut?

By placing it when soft against disks or wheels of iron or copper, supplied with emery; they are kept constantly turning, and, by rubbing against the glass, cut it into whatever shape is required. By the same method the surface is polished.

Is any thing ever used besides emery?

If the cutting is not to be of the best kind, sand and water are substituted for the emery. Sometimes stone wheels are used instead of metal.

If the first cutting is rough what is done?

The marks of it are removed by wooden wheels fed with pumice and rotten stone, and finally by applying a preparation of tin and lead, called putty powder.

How are glass globes and lamp shades polished inside?

Sand is placed in each globe, and by means of a machine they are made to revolve very rapidly. The friction of the sand making the glass perfectly smooth.

Were the lenses of flint-glass used in telescopes at first like those we now have?

No; they were very small and had many defects.

How were the improvements made in them?

Many experiments were tried by different persons without success. At length M. Guinaud, a Swiss clock-maker, accomplished the work.

How was it done?

By stirring the mixture in the melting pots when it was hottest, and while gradually cooling.

How large are lenses now made?

Those of Flint glass are 29 inches, and of Crown glass 20 inches in diameter. But before this improvement they were only about $3\frac{1}{2}$ inches.

What use is made of these lenses ?

They are mostly for telescopes.

What is a lens ?

It is a piece of glass, shaped like a bean. The word lens coming from the Latin " *lentil*," which means *a bean.*

Are all lenses of the same form ?

No ; some have both the edges curved in, others bulge out; or one edge will be straight, while the other is curved. There are many different forms as you will see by the figures below.

CHAPTER IV.

GLASS ORNAMENTS, ETC.

How are glass beads made?

The mixture is prepared as for window glass, and when blown into the globe form, while one workman is still holding it, another having on his *pontil* a piece of melted glass, fastens it to the end of the globe directly opposite the blow-pipe.

What is then done?

As quickly as possible, the two men separate from each other, drawing the melted glass after them in the form of a tube, all the time whirling it round so that it may not lose its shape.

How long is the tube?

It is 100 or 150 ft. in length. This depends upon the size the beads are to be made. If they are very small, of course the glass is drawn into a very long and fine tube, but if not, it is much shorter and larger.

What is the next process ?

The tubes are divided into pieces, about 30 inches long. Each is then cut, by means of an anvil, into the length required for the beads.

What prevents the little tubes from closing while they are yet hot ?

As soon as the beads are cut, they are thrown into a mixture of sand and wood ashes, to which a little water has been added and by means of a machine kept in motion ; the holes in the beads are then filled up.

Is any thing else done with them ?

Yes ; they must be polished.

In what manner ?

As soon as the beads are cold, they are placed in a hollow vessel ; sand is then added, which, by the constant motion of the vessel, rubs against the beads and makes them perfectly smooth. The mixture with which they were filled is removed, and they are now ready for sale.

How are glass paper weights made ?

Pieces of colored filigree glass, representing flowers birds, etc., are placed within the globes while they are still hot, which the workman make to collapse or close over the figures by drawing in his breath, which takes all the air out.

Are the flowers, etc., really as large as they seem to be ?

No ; they are much smaller ; but the shape of the covering magnifies them.

How is the filigree formed?

By melting different colored glass rods against hot lumps partly shaped into bottles, decanters, etc. A little skill on the part of the workman can turn them into many beautiful figures.

How is glass colored?

By adding various ingredients to the mixture. All the colors can be formed from oxide of iron—that is, oxygen combined with iron.

Upon what does the brightness of the colors depend?

It depends upon the intensity of the heat. The greatest degree produces the most brilliant colors.

Does the color always extend through all the glass?

No ; sometimes only the outside is colored.

How is this done?

By dipping the soft clear glass, after it has been shaped upon the *marver*, into a pot of the melted colored mixture then blowing it to the shape required, or opening it out into panes as we have before described.

If the color should be too deep, how is the defect remedied?

By grinding the glass down until it appears lighter.

Sometimes we see clear colorless figures in blue, green, and red cups, dishes, etc. How is this done?

By cutting through the outside down to the uncolored part beneath.

What is enamelled glass?

It is a very beautiful kind of glass, on which figures appear as if cut in the vase or urn itself, or laid on very carefully.

Explain the process for making it.

The material of which it is made, is ground to the very finest powder, formed into a paste, and then laid with a brush upon the glass

How are the figures formed ?

After the enamelling dries, the figures are carved out, either by hand or a machine. The articles are then placed in a furnace and exposed to very great heat, until the enamel has become vitrified.

What is the meaning of vitrified ?

Changed into glass.

What is then done ?

The sheets of glass, or whatever may have been enamelled, are placed in a large kiln to be annealed. About a week from the commencement is required to complete the work.

Can glass be formed into any shape when it is cold ?

No ; because it is so very brittle. But while warm it can be blown or moulded into any form.

How thin may it be made ?

Glass can be blown as thin as soap bubbles, so as to float in the air. It may also be drawn into very fine threads several hundred feet long.

Is any use made of this glass thread ?

It is sometimes woven with silk, forming beautiful materials for dress and fancy articles.

Is glass used for any other purposes than those already mentioned ?

Yes ; within a few years it has been applied to

buildings and different things, in the form of a coating, thereby rendering them fire-proof.

How is the solution made?

The glass mixture is composed of equal parts of silica
and caustic potash. This can be dissolved in boiling
water, and is then ready for use. Cloth dipped in it
will also become fire-proof.

*How are the beautiful figures made which we see painted
on glass?*

Each color is mixed separately with substances
that will melt more readily than those used for glass ;
boiled oil is then added, and the colors are laid on as
in ordinary painting with a brush, or stamped with
blocks as calico is printed.

*What prevents the figures from fading or being washed
off?*

The glass is heated, when the colors sink in and
are made *fast.*

Did the ancients understand how to paint glass?

Yes ; they were very skillful, being able to do it
much better than people now-a-days. Their receipts
for making the colors are still preserved, but the
method of using them is unknown.

SECTION III.

CHAPTER I.

POTTERY AND PORCELAIN.

Are Pottery and Porcelain new inventions ?

No ; the art of making vessels in clay, and baking them in the sun or by fire has been known from the earliest ages.

How far back do the ancients trace the beginning of this art ?

They say there is no account of its commencement in their records, so they conclude it must have been the work of their gods who gave it to men.

What other reason do they give for this belief ?

The fact that different nations, widely separated, and having no way of communicating with each other, all understood how to make these earthen vessels, confirmed them in that opinion.

Did the ancients make any use of Pottery except for household articles ?

Yes ; they made them into sheets or slabs, on which

were inscribed in hieroglyphics, any remarkable events they -wished to preserve. The walls of their tombs were used for a similar purpose.

What are hieroglyphics ?

It means word-painting, or picture-writing. Before letters and writing were known, the account of any event was expressed by certain pictures ; these were called hieroglyphics.

Give an example.

If the description of a battle was required, the whole scene was either drawn or painted. Certain objects also represented certain ideas.

What were some of these objects ?

The figure of a lion or bear denoted courage ; that of a fox, cunning. An eagle, nobility of birth, character and strength of body ; a circle, eternity, because it has neither beginning or end ; an ostrich feather expressed truth ; a lighted lamp denoted life ; and so of many other things.

What nations employed hieroglyphics ?

All those that had made any progress in civilization.

Can we now understand the meaning of this picture-writing ?

By long study and close examination, very skillful persons are able to do so.

What have we learned thereby ?

Many important things concerning the early settlement, manners and customs, wonderful events, etc., of the different nations, which we could not have otherwise known.

Was the Pottery of the ancients very beautiful?

Yes; some of it was, although their earlier specimens were very plain and common.

Have any improvements been made in the art?

Yes, many; although the potter's wheel and furnace now in use, differ very little from those of the oldest nations.

In what countries do we find earthen-ware most commonly used?

In Asia, and parts of Africa, especially Egypt, where nearly every article seems to be made of it, if at all possible.

Mention some of the purposes for which it is used?

For the household; articles for religious and funeral ceremonies; and in cases where we would have boxes, baskets, casks, bottles, etc., stone jars, jugs, vases and urns are substituted.

Of what size and shape are they made?

They are of all sizes, from seven or eight feet high down to hardly an inch, and of every shape to suit the purposes for which they were intended

What articles were more generally formed by the ancients than any other?

Water jars, because pumps were unknown to them, and all the water was carried in jars from the wells, which were often some distance from their house or tent.

Why did not every family have a well?

Either because they were too poor, or moved about

from place to place so frequently that they would not take the trouble to make them.

How many of these water jars would one person carry at once?

Sometimes three, one in each hand and a third on the head.

How were they made?

Some had short, wide necks, others with narrow openings and a spout at the side.

For what did they use the earthen jars in their houses?

For wine, oil, milk, honey, drugs, ointments, grains, fruits, vegetables, etc. The vessel for each article being different from those used for other purposes.

How was it with those designed for religious rites?

They also differed from all the others, and were regarded as so sacred that they could never be taken for any thing else.

In their funeral ceremonies what do we find?

Vases, jars, and urns unlike any of those we have mentioned.

For what were they intended?

To hold the flowers, fruit and other offerings which they placed upon the graves, or in the tombs of their friends.

What did they regard the most precious of all?

The urns in which they kept their ashes.

Did they not bury the dead as we do?

No; the ancients burned their bodies, then carefully gathered the ashes, and placed them in urns or jars.

Where were these kept?

In their tombs or houses.

Were the bodies of the dead always burned?

No ; they were often embalmed, as we have already explained.

Were the mummies placed in earthen cases?

Yes ; after the body had been wrapped in cloths, etc. There were also vases used for holding parts of the body removed in embalming. They never allowed any portion to be lost, because they believed the soul and body would be again united, and if any part was wanting the union would not be perfect.

Were any other articles used in the burial of their dead?

Yes ; urns and jars different from any of the others were placed in the tombs to hold food and such things as they might need, for it was believed the departed wandered about for some time before reaching their final resting-place.

Of what were the jars, etc., made?

The usual materials for glazed ware, were soda and sand, colored with different metals combined with oxygen.

How has time affected these colors?

Although 4000 years have passed away since many of the articles were made, yet they are now as bright as at first.

Can you tell how some of the colors are formed for Glass and Pottery?

Dark blue is obtained by using oxygen and cobalt, which is a reddish-gray or grayish-white metal.

For sky-blue, oxygen and copper. For ruby-red, oxygen and gold, and so of the other colors.

Was the glazed ware of all nations equally good?

No ; that of the Egyptians excelled the Assyrians. The Babylonian Pottery was similar to the Assyrian. The latter made beads and bracelets in great quantities ; also bricks, tiles, tablets, etc., all of earthen ware, on which were inscribed the names of their kings and any remarkable events necessary to be recorded. These with other documents formed the libraries of the ancient nations.

What other use was made of baked clay ?

Images of various kinds were formed of it to represent their gods, famous men, etc. The largest of these were then covered with brass or bronze. Those which they valued or honored the most were coated with gold or silver.

What did they sometimes use for their buildings ?

The largest and most magnificent were built of bricks covered with *these different metals.*

CHAPTER II.

ETRUSCAN WARE.

Why is Etruscan ware so called?

Because it was first made in Etruria, one of the ancient divisions of Italy.

How long since it began to be used there?

More than 2500 years.

How does it differ from other Pottery?

It is a coarse, brown ware, having raised figures of different colors, yet so beautiful as to be classed among the works of art.

Did the Etruscan ware undergo any change?

For a long time it remained the same, but when the Etrurians began to associate with the Greeks, early in the 5th century, B.C. greater variety was seen in it. Instead of brown terra-cotta, black, red, yellow, and other colors appeared.

What is terra cotta?

The words are from the Italian and mean "*Baked Clay.*" When we speak of terra-cotta, we mean the earthen ware on which raised or painted figures are seen. Vases, fancy cups, and other ornamental objects are made of it.

How has the most ancient Etruscan ware been preserved for so long a time ?

We owe this preservation to the custom of the people, which was to bury vases and various articles made of it, with their dead in sepulchres and catacombs.

Was it used for any thing else ?

Yes. Even the tombs were sometimes made of this ware.

Are any now to be seen ?

They are occasionally found among ancient ruins. Two slabs of Etruscan ware are preserved as curiosities in the British Museum.

What may be seen on these slabs ?

At the ends and on the side are raised figures. The cover is ornamented with the full-length figure of an Etruscan female.

Are there any other specimens in the Museum ?

Yes ; there is a very beautiful vase, on which is represented an Etruscan cottage, with a movable door and vaulted roof.

For what was it probably used ?

It doubtless held the ashes of some distinguished person. It was found placed in a larger two-handled vase, so that when buried in the earth, it would remain uninjured.

Have improvements been constantly made in this kind of ware?

Not so much as in many other things. The articles manufactured after the 3d century, B.C., were not so beautiful as before that time.

What was the cause of this?

When Alexander the Great, King of Macedon, had conquered many other countries, he obtained so much silver, gold and precious stones, that he caused vases, urns, etc., to be made or ornamented with them instead of clay.

What is Porcelain?

The best kind of earthen-ware is called Porcelain.

Where was it first made?

China and Japan are supposed to have been the countries where this art originated, having been used there at least since A.D. 442.

What use was made of it?

It was employed for domestic purposes, also for slabs and tiles to cover buildings.

What remarkable building in China is ornamented in this way?

The famous Pagoda or Temple at Nankin ; it was destroyed by fire in 1856. The porcelain manufactured in this city is of the finest quality ; the business being more extensively carried on here than elsewhere.

From what is the name Porcelain derived?

Some authors tell us it is so called from its resemblance to a shell called *Porcellana.* Others say that it is formed from the French words *"Pour cent années,"* which means " For a hundred years,"—because it was formerly believed necessary for the materials to remain under ground for 100 years, before they could be used, but of course this is not the case.

Which of the two theories then can we believe ?

The first is more probably correct. There is still another which derives the word from *porcella*—meaning a " *little cup."*

What progress did the people of China make in this art?

Their success was so great that Marco Polo, who travelled through the country in the 13th century, relates that he found China-ware so cheap and abundant, he could purchase eight beautiful cups for a groat, which is about four pence in English money, making them only a cent a piece in our currency

Did the Chinese make known their art to other nations ?

No ; for they are so exceedingly jealous of foreigners that they would not export the best specimens, fearing the secret of making them might be found out.

How was it at last known ?

A cunning Frenchman succeeded in learning the art, and was not long in making good use of it.

When do we first hear of it in Europe?

In 1531 ; but it was not until 1712 that the art of manufacturing it was known.

What name is given to the choicest kind of this ware?

It is called " *Crackle."*

Why is this term used?

Because the glazing is covered with a net-work of cracks, caused by a sudden cooling of the ware at a certain part of the baking.

What is then done with the cups?

They are washed in a colored glazing, sometimes ruby red, which fills the cracks, giving them a very beautiful appearance.

What other variety of Porcelain can you mention?

There is another more beautiful even than the preceding. In this, the color of the cup is only brought out when it is filled with a liquid.

Explain how this is done.

The design or figure is painted on the inner surface of a very thin cup. It is then washed over with a delicate coating of the paste, so that the figures are enclosed between the inner and outer surface. The liquid acts as a kind of background, preventing the light from passing through, so the figures can be seen.

What is then done?

The vase or cup is baked as usual, after which the latter surface is ground down nearly to the colored figures, and then glazed.

Is this easily done?

No; it is a delicate operation and requires the most skillful workmen to do it successfully.

What other kind of China can you mention?

The variety known as Egg-shell ware. It was so

pure and delicate as to be almost transparent, and sometimes as thin as bamboo paper.

What colors were generally used for it?

White, cream-color, or an exquisite blue, which was obtained from Cobalt.

Did they make much use of cobalt?

Yes; it was employed so much in coloring, that in the year 1500 the Chinese had exhausted their supply.

How have they since obtained what they require?

From Europe, and the greater part from England.

What other nations understood the art of making porcelain?

The Japanese. It was known by them as early, and carried on as successfully, as by the Chinese. The natives of South and Central America were also very skillful, also the "mound-builders" of the West.*

---

* When and by whom those mounds were built has puzzled the busy brains of more than one wise man. They are found scattered through various parts of the United States. But the valley of the Ohio river seems to have been a favorite place for their erection. Probably the mild climate, beautiful scenery, and fertile soil, were as great inducements *then as now* for settlers to make their homes in that part of the country. On account of the dry seasons for the past two years, the Ohio river has been much lower than was ever known before. In consequence of this, a portion of the bed has been exposed to view more clearly. This is at Smith's Ferry, where the Pennsylvania line crosses the Ohio. Here a ledge of rock from 50 to 100 feet wide, and several hundred yards long, is exposed to view. It is covered with inscriptions, such as are usually attributed to the people that dwelt here before the present race of Indians. If this can be interpreted they will doubtless throw

How does the ware made by the Peruvians differ from that of other nations ?

The clay was usually red or yellow, and ornamented with figures in various colors.

much light upon the early nations that peopled this country. Near Aberdeen, on the Ohio side of the river, are two large earth mounds, in the shape of a cone, about 30 feet high and 150 in circumference at the base. They are nearly 400 feet apart, and covered with large trees, which, according to the usual estimate, must be at least 600 years old. These mounds are not yet opened, but for various reasons they are supposed to have been used as sepulchers. This opinion seems the more reasonable, as a mound on the opposite side of the river was opened a few years ago and found to contain several skeletons. The same is true of some of the small rock mounds near Maysville, Ky. The bones taken from them, either crumbled to dust, or broke n pieces when removed. It is not known how long bones can ·emain buried without being entirely decomposed. If this could be ascertained, then we might be able to tell the age of the rock-mounds. Each grave usually contained two or more skeletons, and was about six feet long, four feet wide, and two deep. It extended from north to south, instead of east to west, as is the custom of the present race of Indians. Ruins of ancient fortifications are also found near Mayslick, Ky.; and not far from Germantown, in the same county, may be seen a very curious excavation, 10 feet deep and 100 feet square. Flat rock covers the floor ; seats appear to have been placed around the wall. Many suppose this to have been an Indian Council Chamber, although there are no certain proofs of it. Various curious utensils of clay and metal have been found here ; they differ entirely from those discovered among the ruins in other parts of the world.

We are indebted to the Louisville *Journal* for much of the information contained in the above note.

What articles were most common among them ?

Drinking vessels and flasks are more generally found, the latter being made with two necks.

What was the object in having two necks ?

Probably that the air might pass in at one opening while the liquid flowed out of the other.

How were the flasks formed?

Many of them were shaped very beautifully, having long delicate necks, or ornamented with the head of the Jaguar or other animals ; some also had the form of birds, and native fruits or flowers. In rare cases, the human face is represented.

How does the pottery of the people of Peru now compare with that of their ancestors ?

It is very inferior, both in form and quality.

In what part of South America are the greatest quantities of crockery made?

In Brazil: the amount manufactured there is so enormous, that sometimes cargoes of boats are seen, composed almost entirely of the "*talhas,*" or large drinking vessels.

Of what are the talhas made?

They are formed of a light, red, porous clay; are unglazed, and will hold about ten or fifteen gallons each.

What can you say of the pottery of Central America ?

In the ruins of this country are often found fine specimens of earthen-ware, well made, beautifully or-namented, and covered with a glazing resembling glass.

*Did the people learn this method of glazing from the Euro-
pains ?*

No; it was probably their own invention, as the art
was not known in Europe for several centuries after
those earlier nations are supposed to have lived in
Central America.

*In what other places have remains of earthen-ware been
found ?*

In Mexico; the specimens there being even more
beautiful than those of Europe. In New Mexico, also,
they are found in the greatest abundance.

What are frequently seen in the Western Mounds ?

Beautiful pipe-bowls moulded in clay in the forms of
animals and birds that are now not found nearer than
the Gulf of Mexico: others represented the human
head. The best pipes were carved in stone.

*How do the vases from the Ohio Mounds seem to have
been hardened ?*

They appear to have been baked over a fire instead
of burned in a kiln.

4

CHAPTER III.

VARIETIES IN POTTERY AND PORCELAIN.

What nation introduced the art of making pottery into Spain ?

The Arabs, when they conquered the country in the early part of the eighth century ; and also into Sicily in the next century.

To what use was their pottery applied ?

The walls of buildings were decorated with it ; also tiles for pavements were made.   In the former they excelled particularly.

How was the pottery used on the buildings ?

It was made into large slabs, covered with cream-colored enamel, highly polished. This was ornamented with beautiful designs in gay colors.

What two famous buildings were adorned in this way ?

The splendid palace of the Spanish kings, called " The Alhambra," and the great Mosque at Palermo.

What improvement took place in the fourteenth century ?

The celebrated Majolica ware was then made.

Why was it so called?

It is supposed the name was given from the island of Majorca, where the Moors had formerly made it.

How is this ware made?

A smooth, white surface is overlaid upon the common clay foundation and then baked in the kiln.

Were any improvements made in it?

Yes, a great many ; they are especially due to Messrs. Robbins, of Florence, who were so skillful in the manufacture of it, that for at least two centuries the Majolica ware was the most celebrated in Europe.

What are its peculiarities?

The articles made of it had a very delicate enamel on the surface.   But its fame was chiefly owing to the beautiful designs that appeared.

Who were employed to paint them?

The most distinguished artists.   In consequence of this, the ware became very expensive, and at length was bought more for the famous pictures, than for the various articles upon which they were painted.

What other European nations excelled in the making of pottery?

The Dutch and French.   The famous Dutch tiles for chimney-pieces, sideboards, etc., are well known. In the houses of the wealthy these were very beautiful, being ornamented with designs by celebrated artists.

What were represented on them?

Sometimes a succession of Scripture scenes, great events in the history of Germany or other countries, etc.

When was Porcelain generally used in Europe ?

After the 16th century we find it becoming more common, until it was a general article of trade.

What improvements were made in England ?

In 1760 Josiah Wedgewood made a beautiful cream-colored ware, which, in honor of Queen Charlotte, he was allowed to call " Queen's ware."

What else did he do ?

He imitated, in porcelain, famous Cameos, precious stones carved into figures, etc., so exactly, that it was almost impossible to distinguish them from the original.

What can you say of his imitation of the celebrated Portland Vase ?

He produced fifty copies of this, which were regarded as beautiful as the original.

What was the Portland Vase ?

This was a very beautiful Vase found in the tomb of Alexander Severus, who died A. D. 235. It is of a deep blue color, having beautiful raised figures in white enamel.

How was that done ?

The art is lost, although, as we have just said, the imitation of Mr. Wedgewood almost equalled the beauty of the Portland Vase itself.

What has been done in the United States in the Pottery business ?

But little attention has been given to it compared with other things.

What is the cause of this ?

It is because we can import the ware so easily and at little expense, that it is not thought a very profitable business.

Are there any materials in this country for making it ?

Yes ; they can be obtained in abundance.

Are there any Potteries here ?

Yes ; in nearly every state several small ones may be found, where the common ware for jugs, jars, etc., is made.

Is Porcelain also manufactured ?

At Jersey City it was made as early as 1816, and afterwards in Philadelphia ; but this establishment closed in 1836.

What variety is produced at Jersey City ?

The cream-colored porcelain ; it is marked, " C. C."

In what other cities is it made?

In New York, Brooklyn, Trenton, Perth Amboy, N. J., Ganesville, East Liverpool, Ohio, East Peoria Ills., etc.

CHAPTER IV

METHOD OF MAKING POTTERY AND PORCELAIN.

What articles are included under the name of Pottery ?

A great variety both in composition, figure and use.

Mention some of them.   `

Bricks and tiles are the coarsest and most common. Then, as the materials, etc., improve in quality, there is a regular gradation from the red earthen-ware, through the varieties of stone-ware up to the various kinds of porcelain.

Into how many classes may Pottery be divided ?

Into four.

What is the first ?

The 1st class includes Soft Pottery, from which arc made bricks, tiles, drain-pipes, chimney-pots, Hessian crucibles, and several varieties of common red ware.

What are found in the 2d class ?

This class embraces fine earthen-ware, made of better materials than the 1st class; it is white and hard, covered with a crystal glazing, containing lead or borax.

Mention the varieties of the 3d class.

In this division are found Stone-ware, both fine and common, the former including the Wedgewood wares.

How does this class differ from real Porcelain ?

It differs in not being translucent, or at least, slightly so, while this is always a quality of Porcelain.

What do you mean by translucent ?

Any thing is translucent when the light passes through it imperfectly—that is, not as clearly as in glass.

How do objects appear when viewed through such a medium ?

They are indistinctly seen.

What do you call glass, water, and such substances as permit rays of light to pass directly through them ?

They are called *transparent.*

What does the 4th class include ?

In this class is found the true Porcelain. It is the hard translucent variety, composed of powdered quartz, feldspar, and very carefully prepared kaolin. After baking it is covered with a peculiar glazing.

What are meant by the terms " hard " and " soft," when applied to Pottery and Porcelain ?

These terms refer to their fusibility—that is, the readiness with which they will burn or melt. The 1st class includes the Soft Pottery, as we have seen, because it is more easily affected by heat. In the last class are found hard wares, upon which fire has little or no power.

Is there always a clear distinction between Pottery and Porcelain ?

The difference, we have stated, is not always observed in speaking of them, as the varieties of each are often found so closely blended. It is on this account that we have given the history of both together.

Upon what do the various kinds of ware depend that are mentioned in the four preceding classes ?

They depend upon the many different mixtures of clays, pulverized quartz, flints, and feldspar, which are minerals. Also upon the coloring matter and glazing materials used.

In making Porcelain and fine earthen-ware, what are used ?

Fine sand, lime, magnesia and alumina—the latter being a kind of clay ; also kaolin and bone-ash.

What is done with these materials ?

They are all powdered very fine and mixed in different quantities for the various kinds of ware to be made, and then kept in the melted state for 48 hours at a very high temperature.

What is then done ?

The glazing mixture is prepared so that the **ware** may hold liquids.

Of what is this made ?

It is composed of different substances ; some of which are fine sand, gypsum, borax, common salt, potash, soda, etc.

How are the various colors produced ?

They are made from oxides of manganese, cobalt, iron, copper, etc.

If enameling is to be made, what are used ?

For enamels, oxide of tin, or a preparation of lime. You will remember when we speak of *an oxide* of *any thing*, we simply mean oxygen united with the tin, iron or other metal.

How is the glazing put on the ware ?

It is made into a paste, which is spread over the porcelain, and then heated, but not so much as when first baked.

In shaping the different articles what method is used ?

When the paste is properly prepared and about as soft as dough or putty, it is worked over and over, by beating, kneading, treading, etc.

Can it be used at once ?

That for the real Porcelain requires more working, and should be stored away moist for at least a year.

Why is this necessary ?

That the dough may go through a molding process, by which it becomes more tender.

What is then done ?

The "*slapping*" process follows. The dough being cut by wire into pieces, these are thrown against each other so as to be thoroughly mixed.

How many methods for shaping the articles ?

There are two. One called " throwing," which is

done by the potter's wheel, and the other " casting "
or " pressing " in molds.

Is the potter's wheel a recent invention ?

Not by any means.   We have already said the kind
now used differs but little from that of the ancient
nations, 2000 B. C.

How is it made ?

A round flat board or metal rests upon an upright
axle. This is turned by a belt from another wheel, by
the hand or foot of the workman applied to a third
wheel, attached below.

How is this simple machine used ?

The potter throws upon the board a lump of clay
cut the exact size of the article he wishes to make,
and as it turns by means of the wheel, he shapes it
with his hand into the form required.

If the article is too small to hold   his hand, what is done ?

He uses some simple tool, as a wet sponge fastened
to a bent stick.

How is the outer part shaped ?

If the article is to be made very exactly, a piece of
metal of the required form is laid over the clay, while
the inner part is shaped by the hand or bent stick

What is sometimes done before completing the vessel ?

A rough form is first given, and then allowed to
dry a little before finishing.

If molds are used, of what are they made ?

Those of gypsum are generally used, as they will
absorb the moisture from the clay

How are the molds used?

Some are single, and shape but one surface; others are double so as to form both the inner and outer part at once. Besides this, molds are sometimes in different pieces so as to shape the parts of the clay-figure separately; these are then joined and baked together.

How is the paste used on the molds?

Frequently it is rolled out, as a baker rolls the dough, then spread over and pressed down on the mold with a wet sponge. This forms the inside of the plate.

How is the outer part made?

It is done by putting the plate and mold on a flat surface; then a thin piece of metal of the required shape is placed above it. The whole is made to revolve, and soon the article is completely formed.

How are handles, spouts, etc., fastened to pitchers, tea-pots, etc.?

Each one is molded separately and fastened by a thin piece of the clay to the main part; both are firmly united when baked. The thin piece is called a "slip."

What takes place after molding?

The vessels are carefully examined, and being placed on the potter's wheel, all the roughness is soon removed.

How are ornamental figures made?

This is accomplished by skillful carving with a knife.

After drying, does the ware come out in good shape ?

Not always; frequently by shrinking unequally it is distorted so as to be useless. Therefore great care is required in this part of the process.

How is it done?

The articles are put on shelves where the heat of the sun or fire may not act directly on them.

Explain the method of baking the ware?

It is placed in drum-shaped clay vessels called " *Seggars*," which being piled on each other fill the kilns.

How are the kilns heated?

By fire which passes through flues on the outside. Of course these kilns are so made as not to be affected by the flame and smoke, as the ware that is placed in them would be discolored.

How long are kilns kept hot?

The time varies with different kinds of ware. The French Porcelain usually requires from 25 to 30 hours.

What is then done?

The kiln is closed for five or eight days, so that the ware may be perfectly annealed.

When taken out, are all the articles perfect?

No ; usually about ¼ are found either out of shape or otherwise injured.

What is done with the others ?

They are finished off with a grinding wheel, etc., which removes any slight defects.

How is the coloring applied?

In various ways, according to the taste of the artist, or the use for which the vessels are designed.

Is the color put on before or after glazing?

Sometimes before, and sometimes after. There are two sorts of colors. One kind is called " refractory," because they will stand the heat of the furnace. These are applied before glazing.

What name is given to the other colors?

They are called " *muffle*," from the kind of furnace in which they are burned. These are added after the ware is baked.

Where is the best porcelain now made?

That at Sévres in France is considered the finest · it bears the name of the city in which it is manufactured.

What prices have been paid for this ware?

Single vases, only 12 or 15 inches high, have often been sold for $5000 ; Majolica plates for $500; Chinese antique vases for $1,500.

What may be seen at the Porcelain Museum of Sévres?

In this collection are found specimens of every kind of ware, from the coarsest to the finest.

Are all of them complete?

Many of them are unfinished in order to show the process of manufacture in all its branches, as well as the great improvements that have been made.

Can a stranger understand the work without a guide?

Yes, perfectly; for each piece is labelled with a

short description of the date, place where it was made, materials employed, and use to which it was applied, etc.

Are most of the specimens of recent date ?

The labels show that they belong to various periods, from the earliest and rudest attempts, to the latest and most finished specimens, so that the whole history of Pottery and Porcelain may be read in this Museum at Sévres.

SECTION IV.

CHAPTER I.

PAPER.

As we examine the different inventions and discoveries of man, do we find all of equal importance ?

By no means; some are of but little use, while others are almost indispensable to our comfort.

What rank may be given to the invention of paper ?

It is *one* of the first, if not the *very first* in importance.

Can you give any reasons for this ?

The more *useful* any thing is, the more we value it, and paper being applied to so many different purposes, it becomes, of course, very valuable.

Will you mention some of the uses for which it is made ?

We find it most necessary in printing and writing : it is also used for covering the walls of rooms, and boxes, wrapping goods, etc.

Are there many varieties ?

Yes, very many ; as bank-note, tissue, cartridge, filtering, blotting, etc.

Is the art of making paper as old as other inventions ?

It is not supposed to be, although we are unable to give the exact date of it.

What was used instead of paper ?

The skins of animals, very carefully dressed, called parchment, was a substitute for paper.

How was it used ?

The writing generally appeared only on one side, but as the parchment was very valuable, the same piece could be used several times by erasing the previous writing.

When and by what nation was it first adopted ?

We are not certain upon this point, as various authors disagree regarding it, but it is known to have been used at least 1400 B.C., by the Egyptians.

What have sometimes been found in the tombs of the ancients ?

Frequently rolls of leather—more or less carefully dressed—are taken out, on which are inscribed the name, age, etc., of the person buried, with the date of his death, and any remarkable events connected therewith

Is parchment still used ?

Yes, to some extent, because nothing else has been found as a substitute.

For what purposes ?

The finer kind, called vellum, is employed for important writings, as deeds, wills, diplomas, etc.

From what is it made?

From the skins of calves, kids, and sometimes lambs.

Is there a coarser kind?

Yes; and that is more generally called parchment, being used for drum-heads.

From what is that made?

The skins of goats, wolves, and asses are chiefly used for the purpose.

Can you tell me the process for making parchment?

All the hair is first removed from the skin; it is then thrown into a lime-pit, to cleanse the grease; after this it must be stretched in a frame, so fixed as to draw the skin as tightly as possible that there may be no wrinkles.

What is next done?

A workman takes a sharp knife shaped something like a sickle, and pares away any pieces of flesh that may still adhere to the skin; then turning the frame over, scrapes off the dirt, lime, etc., on the other side.

How is the surface smoothed?

Sifted chalk, or slaked lime is scattered on the inner side, and rubbed with pumice-stone. The outer is also dressed, but only with the pumice.

Is the skin dried very quickly?

No; quite gradually, and in summer it must be moistened occasionally that it may dry slowly enough. In winter great care is taken to guard it against the frost.

What is the next operation ?

When thoroughly dried and stretched, the skin is removed from the frame, and pared down about half its thickness, and again rubbed with pumice.

How is the smooth polish given to it ?

This is done by brushing it over with the white of an egg, or solution of gum arabic.

What was formerly used besides parchment ?

From the earliest ages *papyrus*—which is the Latin word for paper—has been made in great quantities.

Why is it so called ?

It is a name given to certain kind of plants that grow in marshy places and also in clear water, from which the papyrus for paper is made.

In what countries is it found ?

The nut-grass in our Southern States, and also the common bulrush, which the poorer people of England use for candle-wicks by burning the pith, are specimens of it.

Is papyrus for making paper like the above ?

It differs somewhat, being found on the marshy banks of rivers in Syria, Sicily, and Abyssinia. The plant was formerly very abundant on the borders of the river Nile, but it is doubtful whether any can now be found in Egypt

Was it valued in that country ?

Yes ; it was greatly esteemed, not only for paper which was made from it, but also for many other uses, to which it was applied.

What were some of them ?

It was employed for medical purposes, especially in the cure of ulcers, etc. ; also torches and candles, boat-sails, ropes, mats, garments, coverlets, shoes for the priests, etc., were manufactured from it.

Were the roots of any use?

Yes ; being as large as a man's arm, they were good for fuel ; cups and other articles were also made of them. The plant was even used for food, being eaten raw, boiled or roasted ; the sweet juice of it, however, was the only part to be swallowed.

How was the papyrus made into paper ?

The stem was divided by a fine needle into thin plates as large as the plant would make. These were spread on a table which was moistened with Nile water. Across these other similar sheets were laid.

Of what use was the water ?

It dissolved the slimy substance in the plant, and made the sheets stick close together, when laid under a heavy press.

What was then done ?

The sheets were hung up in the sun to dry, and afterwards rolled on a wooden cylinder.

Is papyrus still used for paper?

No ; for a long time it has ceased to be employed for that purpose. It was gradually disappearing in the 11th and 12th centuries, when cotton and linen began to be substituted for it.

Where are rolls of papyri often found?

They may be seen in nearly all the mummy cases.

For what purpose were they placed there ?

As the hieroglyphic characters on all of them are nearly the same, it is supposed they were intended as a sort of passport, which the bearer could present for admission into the other world.

Have any important sheets of Papyri been found recently ?

Yes ; a Frenchman named Mariette Bey discovered 150 rolls at Memphis in Egypt, giving much valuable information regarding the religion and government of the country.

CHAPTER II.

EARLY HISTORY OF PAPER.

How long has paper been made from linen and cotton?

This is not certainly known. In Europe we find it first used in the 10th and 11th centuries, as we have already said. But the art seems to have been understood in other countries long before this.

By what nations was it made?

By the Arabians and Persians, who probably introduced it into Europe. The people in other parts of Asia also produce it from various materials.

What have the Chinese done?

The art among them is very ancient; each province having its own peculiar kind of paper.

What materials do they use?

Sometimes the inner bark of trees, which is formed into a pulp and worked into paper. It is said that in the province of Se-chuen they made it of linen rags as in Europe; and in Fo-kein the young bamboo is used for the same purpose.

How is it made from this plant?

The portion to be used is cut into pieces several feet long, and soaked in water for several days, then dried by covering it with slaked lime.

What is the next process?

After drying, it is thoroughly washed, cut into strips, dried again and bleached in the sun, then boiled in water, and beaten to a pulp in a wooden mortar.

What is now added?

The solution of a certain gum is mixed with the pulp by beating it again in mortars. After this the whole is poured into tubs.

Is it now ready to form into paper?

Yes; and this is done by a workman who takes out enough for a sheet of the size he wishes to make. This is placed in a mould to be shaped and partly dried.

What then follows?

The drying is finished by placing the sheets on hot air pipes, and the final smoothness given to the paper by dipping in a solution of alum.

Are the Japanese as skillful as the Chinese in making paper?

Yes; and even more so. That which they manufacture is so strong and durable, that it can be used for many purposes to which cloth is applied.

What does it resemble?

Some of it looks so much like silk and cotton, that it is almost impossible to tell them apart.

What can you say of the origin, etc., of paper from cotton and linen?

Gibbon, the English historian, says that the art was carried to Samarcand from China in the year 651, and to Mecca in 707.

Was linen first used in making it?

No; it is generally supposed that cotton was taken before linen.

In what country do we find much paper made from linen?

In two provinces of Spain, where flax and hemp are raised in great quantities.

What is the oldest specimen of linen paper in that country?

The one bearing the earliest date, 1178, is a treaty of peace between Arragon and Spain.

When was the art introduced in to other countries?

In France in 1314; about the same time into Germany. Fifty years later we find it in Italy. It was used in England in the reign of Edward II., although not very extensively, the people seeming still to prefer parchment or vellum.

When was it first manufactured there?

It was made to some extent in the time of Henry VII., but the first great manufactory was carried on by John Spielman, a German, who was the jeweller to Queen Elizabeth.

Was enough then made for the use of the people?

No; for the progress of the business was so slow, that

even in the 17th century, the English were obliged to
obtain much from France.

What at length caused a change for the better ?

On account of troubles in the government of France
many of the people, called refugees, were obliged to
leave that country. They fled to England, bringing
with them some of the trades of their own country,
among which paper-making was then one of the most
important.

Did they excel in the art ?

Yes ; the paper made by them was considered the
best, and we find the exiles carrying on the business
very extensively in England, then their adopted country.

What kind of paper was made at first ?

It was nearly all *brown*. But in 1690 special
attention was given to the manufacture of the
white.

Did any changes take place in Germany ?

After using linen and cotton for some time, in 1756,
they first attempted making paper from straw, and
afterwards from the bark of the linden or bass-wood
tree.

*Can you mention any improvement among the
French ?*

The sheets had been limited in size, but in 1798
Louis Robert announced that he had invented a
machine by which rolls of it could be made 12 feet wide
and 50 feet long. This was doubtless the first step
towards manufacturing wall-paper.

Soon after, what change in the materials took place in England?

Matthias Koops, in 1800, produced 100 reams of good white paper per week, from old waste pieces which had either been written or printed before.

What else did he use?

He made better paper from straw, wood, and other vegetable products, than had yet been produced from any materials.

As we turn now to our own country, when do we find the first paper-mill established here?

The earliest of which we have any account, was erected in 1714 upon Chester Creek, Del. Mr. Wilcox, who afterwards bought it, furnished Benjamin Franklin with all that he used in his printing establishment.

What can you say of this mill?

It is still in operation and owned by a son of Mr. Wilcox. The process of making paper by hand, as it was done a century ago, may yet be seen there.

Could the materials for making it be readily obtained?

No; the demand for paper soon became so great that it was impossible to supply the orders received.

What was one cause of this?

People had not yet formed the habit of saving the waste scraps of cotton or linen, and even though carts went round to collect them, it seemed difficult to obtain what was needed.

What effort was made to increase the supply?

Premiums were offered for any person who would

make the greatest quantity of paper from other materials than rags.

Did this remove the trouble ?

Not entirely, for it was found necessary to import
rags from Europe, Italy and Austria, furnishing
at least three-fourths of the whole amount shipped.

*How were the machines for making paper worked at
first ?*

The simplest form was by hand ; then horse-powei
was employed, and in 1816, at Pittsburgh, steam began to be used.

*What part of the material was taken in the early
days of paper making ?*

Only the finest and best ; but, as improvements
were made in cleansing and bleaching, the coarser
parts could also be used.

Did the demand still continue ?

It was constantly increasing, so that in 1852 more
paper was consumed in the U. S. than in France and
England together.

*What materials are now found suitable for making
the article ?*

All those vegetable substances that can be turned
into pulp by being crushed and mixed with water.

Which seem best adapted for the purpose ?

Nothing has been found more suitable than flax
and cotton ; and they can be more readily used,
when in the form of rags, than in the raw material,
or when just woven.

Why is this so ?

By the constant wearing and washing of the cloth, the rags are already half prepared for forming paper, as they will be more easily converted into pulp.

Can paper be made very quickly ?

Yes ; by the great improvements of the day, rags can be shipped in the morning several miles, and manufactured into paper before night.

What objection to this method of making it ?

It has been found that paper turned out so rapidly is not as strong and durable as if more time had been employed.

Can you mention any other improvements besides those already given ?

It was supposed that white paper could only be made from cotton and linen rags, at least the kind used for writing and printing, while the cheap brown wrapping-paper was manufactured from the coarser materials, as old ropes, and the waste from cotton mills.

What are the facts now ?

The finest white, and even delicate tissue paper can be made from both coarse and fine materials : an excellent article is now produced from the cane found so abundantly in the Southern swamps, also from hemlock and bass-wood; the latter is not however considered as good a material as some others.

How was the cane formed into pulp ?

The process proved at first slow and difficult, as it was necessary to boil it in a strong solution of alkali and then bleach it.

How is the work now done ?

A curious American invention accomplished it much more easily. The long canes were put into a very strong iron cylinder, so as to bear great pressure from the steam which was forced in.

What effect was produced by this ?

The result was similar to that of powder shot from a gun.

Explain it.

On opening one end of the cylinder, the power of the steam was so great that it forced the cane out very suddenly, tearing it into fine threads.

Did any thing remain ?

Yes ; around the cylinder the hard outer covering of the cane was crushed into a white, pure mass of material ready to be formed into pulp.

Has this machine been applied to any thing else ?

Logs of bass or white wood have been successfully treated in the same way.

What may be seen at the Smithsonian Institute ?

The copy of a work written by Schäffer, a German, in 1772, upon the various ways of making paper out of other materials than rags.

What is there remarkable about this book ?

It is printed on more than sixty kinds of paper formed from as many different substances.

What other curious work can you mention ?

The writings of the Marquis de Villette, published in London in 1786, are printed on paper made of marsh-mallow.

What is at the end of the book ?

There are single leaves, made at Bruges, of 20 species of plants, as nettles, hops, moss, reed, various kinds of trees, herbs, etc.

How many materials have thus far been used in making paper ?

One author mentions 103 substances, mostly vegetable, with a few mineral and animal.

What do we learn from all this ?

That many objects in nature, which appear almost worthless, have been found among the most useful.

Has every natural production been used for some purpose ?

No ; there are many things that yet seem useless to us, but in time will doubtless be found very valuable.

Why have we reason to think so?

Discoveries of that kind are being constantly made: and for a still better reason, because Almighty God has some wise design in every thing He makes, even the vilest insect, as well as the smallest vegetable and mineral product.

CHAPTER III.

METHOD OF MAKING PAPER.

In the manufacture of paper are the raw materials ready for use ?

By no means : so that it is at first necessary to prepare them ; of course different methods are required for the various materials.

If rags are used what is the process ?

One method is the following : The rags are first cut into narrow strips by women seated at a table, the top being covered with a net-work which allows the dust to fall through.

Is a machine used for cutting them ?

The only machine is a knife blade fastened upright to the table ; across this the rags are cut. The buttons, hooks and eyes being laid aside, also silk and woollen pieces.

After cutting, where are the rags placed ?

They are thrown into a large box near the table, which is divided into several parts to receive them according to their quality, etc. ; all the loose dirt is then shaken out by a machine.

What is next done ?

The rags are carried to the boiler, which is partly filled with a solution of different substances, that all the color may be taken out of them. Sometimes very strong lye is required for this purpose, also soda.

Is the lye used for any thing else ?

Yes ; it will dissolve the hard rough particles that are often found, which if not removed would make uneven places in the paper. It also washes out much of the dirt remaining on the rags.

Is the solution warm or cold ?

It is warm. The best method for heating all parts equally is by means of steam pipes. The round boilers, being placed on their side, are made to revolve so that the lye is constantly working through the whole of the mixture.

Why is this necessary ?

If it were not done, some portions being cleansed and bleached more than the rest, the paper would come out discolored and imperfect.

How much can be put in the boilers at once?

Several hundred weight of rags are boiled together. Then steam at a high pressure is applied, which hastens the work.

How long does this process continue ?

It is usually finished in about 8 or 10 hours.

What now takes place?

The rags are next converted into pulp.

How was this formerly done ?

The rags were placed in stone vats where they remained for several weeks, and by the aid of heat and moisture would ferment, after which they were beaten in wooden mortars.

How were these mortars made ?

There was a cavity in the bottom covered with a thick iron plate, the top of which was grooved, as were also the mallets for pounding.

How was the moisture from the rags carried off ?

By means of a hole in the mortar, which was protected by hair cloth, to prevent the particles from passing through.

What is now used as a substitute for the mortar ?

A machine called the " Engine," invented by the Dutch.

How many of these are required at once ?

Two engines are usually worked together, the " washer " and " beater," both on the same plan.

What is the object of the two ?

One is for cleansing the rags, and the other for rubbing and forming them into pulp.

Are they connected ?

Sometimes the " beater " is placed under the " washer," or each can be used separately ; the latter is the usual method, so that the cleansing may be well done.

How are the rags formed into pulp ?

The " washer " and " beater " each contain a solid cylinder; that in the former has 40 steel bars or ribs running lengthwise, the latter 60. On the floor of the engine, a corresponding set of bars is firmly fixed.

Of what use are the bars?

By the working of the "Engine," the rags are rubbed against them and crushed very fine into pulp, without being actually cut.

Does the machine work very rapidly?

It can easily be made to do so, but it is better to work it more slowly, as the quality of the paper will be thereby improved.

How is water used during the operation?

A constant stream falls into the cylinder at the same time that the dirty water passes out below.

How is it known when the pulp is perfectly formed?

By the motion of the machine.

Explain this more fully.

When the cylinder begins to work the motion is very irregular, moving roughly and by jerks.

To what is this owing?

It is caused by the coarseness of the rags, which do not pass easily between the bars. But as they become gradually crushed, the motion of the engine is more regular, and at length quite steady.

What does this prove?

It shows that the pulp is perfectly formed.

What length of time is required for this process?

The best paper requires three or four hours, although as we have said, it may be done in much less time, but the result is not so satisfactory.

Explain the method of bleaching?

The pulp passes out of the cylinder by means of a

6

pipe to the draining chest, where much of the moisture escapes: it is then put in stone cisterns.

What materials are used for bleaching?

A solution of chloride of lime with about one pound of salt to two gallons of water.

Does this remain in the cistern?

No; for the bottom being made of zinc, perforated with fine holes, the liquid passes through, but by means of a pump is brought up again, when stronger liquor is added.

How long does the pulp remain in the bleaching mixture?

About 24 hours, when it comes out nearly white.

What is now done with the pulp?

Sometimes it is put under a very heavy press, that all the chlorine moisture may be removed, or it is taken directly to the " *beater*," which works like the washing engine already described.

Why is it necessary to remove the chlorine water?

Because if any remains in the pulp, the paper becomes very brittle and will crumble to pieces.

What is now added?

The sizing and coloring matter, unless the paper is to be white.

What is the sizing?

It is a preparation which makes the surface smooth and glossy.

Of what is it composed?

Soda and rosin are mixed together forming a kind of soap, then alum is added, which causes the rosin to unite with the pulp.

How long does the mixture remain in the " beater" ?

The beating operation usually requires from three to four hours, when the pulp passes into a large vat.

What was the method formerly adopted for forming the pulp into sheets ?

It was done almost entirely by hand. The workman took a shallow, mahogany box, called a mold, which was a little larger than the sheet to be made. This was covered with fine wires, and around it was placed a loose frame of the exact size required for the paper.

What was the next step in the process ?

The workman then shook some of the pulp on the wires in such a way that it would spread evenly over them, while the moisture passed through.

What was done with this mold ?

It was passed over to another man called a "coucher," who set it up on edge to dry. He then spread a piece of felt cloth on a table, and turned over the sheet in the mold upon it.

What followed ?

A piece of felt was placed above the sheet of pulp ; and the same process was continued until about 130 sheets were so arranged, each one separated by a piece of felt. They were then put under a heavy press, when much moisture flowed out.

Was the operation then finished ?

No ; much yet remained to be done.

Explain still further.

After remaining under press for some time, the

sheets were taken out separately and piled up by themselves, pressed again, then a second time taken apart and pressed once more.

What was now done?

The paper was hung up on hair lines to dry; this could be done in 24 hours if the weather was favorable. It was then sized by dipping in a preparation of glue and alum.

Was the work now ended?

No; the sheets required another pressure to remove the sizing if there should be too much, and were again hung on the lines to be dried more gradually than before, so that the sizing would thoroughly penetrate the paper.

What was finally done?

The sheets were laid on glazed paper boards and hot metal plates applied through the pile, or smooth copper plates were rolled between the sheets.

What length of time was required for this process?

It was generally three weeks from the time the rags were sorted until the paper was ready for sale, and for every vat, from which almost 150 lbs. could be made, eight men and as many women were employed.

In what time can this same work now be accomplished?

As we have before said, it may all be completed in a single day.

To what are we indebted for this great improvement?

It is owing to the invention of the Fourdrinier machine.

State some of the advantages of this machine.

A much greater quantity can be made in the same time at far less cost. The paper is produced of any size or quality required, either thick, as that for flour bags, or thin, as tissue paper.

Can you mention any other benefits?

The sorting, trimming, drying, etc., is now unnecessary, this having been the longest part of the operation.

Is the paper of as good quality as that made by hand?

Yes; and even superior to it; if the work is not done too quickly, it is also equally strong and durable.

What proof can you give of this?

Mr. Herring, an Englishman, among different kinds of paper, exhibited a specimen which was of the thickness of ordinary letter paper, the piece not larger than a bank note, yet it would bear a weight of 200 lbs.

Will you explain the method of making paper by the Fourdrinier machine?

Before passing into this machine, the rags are sorted, very carefully, cut by machinery, and passed into a rotary boiler holding about two tons; steam being admitted, they are then boiled.

What is done with them now?

They are taken to the lower story and carried by cars to the washing engine, where the cleansing and bleaching process takes place as we have before described.

What is done with the pulp when formed?

It is thrown into an immense vat, which stands at

the head of the Fourdrinier machine, and constantly stirred so that the thickness may be the same throughout.

How is it taken from the vat?

There is a stop-cock at the bottom by means of which the pulp may pass out as required, and according to the thickness of the paper to be made. Sometimes pumps are used, giving out equal quantities in equal portions of time.

What is done with the pulp as it leaves the vat?

It flows upon a "lifter wheel," and is then diluted with water drained from a web of paper.

Of what use is the wheel?

It carries the mixture into a trough called a "sand trap," which is 4 or 5 inches deep and 20 to 40 feet long.

Why is it so called?

Because if any particles of sand still remain in the pulp, they settle to the bottom, and the rest will pass out through the strainer at the side of the trough.

What becomes of the hard, knotty particles that may still remain in the mixture?

They will be caught by the strainer, and only the soft, pure part passes off.

How were they formerly removed?

They were picked out of the paper by hand, while it was drying, many sheets were thereby defective, so that often one in every five would be cast aside as useless.

What becomes of the pulp after leaving the strainer?

It flows into a vat which is as long as the width of the sheet to be made, and then passes out of one side upon the "wire."

What is the wire?

It is an endless web of wire cloth so fine that there are from 3000 to 5000 holes to the square inch.

Upon what does it rest?

The "wire" is supported on rollers, by which it is carried round from 25 to 70 ft. per minute.

What regulates the width of the pulp upon it?

Flexible straps or "*dickles*" are arranged on each side according to the required width of the paper.

Of what are the dickles made?

They are formed of several layers of linen or cotton gummed, or of vulcanized rubber.

What change takes place in the pulp?

As the moisture is gradually pressed out by means of a heavy cylinder under which it passes, the pulp unites more and more closely.

What is often fastened to this roll or cylinder?

Very fine wire, in the form of letters or figures, being sewed to it, the impression is left on the pulp, causing the "*water lines*," as they are called, in the paper.

Are these figures of any use?

Yes ; it is from them that the different names given to paper are known.

Give some examples.

The style of paper known as "cap" or "fool's-cap

was so called from the figure of a fool's cap' and bells appearing in the water lines. "*Post*" *paper* has the design of a postman's horn, etc.

Have these marks been applied to any very useful purpose?

By marking them upon checks, bank-notes, etc., it is much more difficult to counterfeit.

What is done to make these impressions more lasting?

Suction boxes are placed under the web of pulp when the wire figures are applied, these draw out the moisture very quickly, leaving the figures more distinct and durable.

After leaving the suction boxes, what becomes of the paper web?

It passes on to the "couch rolls."

What are these?

They are rollers covered with felt, one of them carrying the wire, while the upper one presses down upon the paper and wire between them.

What is then done?

After being sufficiently pressed, the wire cloth passes back to the trough from which it came, to be used again, while the web passes on to an endless piece of felt.

Is it now dry?

No ; it is still very wet and must therefore be placed with the felt between a pair of very heavy cast iron rollers, so that nearly all the moisture may be pressed out.

Does not the impression of the felt remain upon the web?

It would unless care was taken to remove it.

How is this done?

The web of paper being now able to support itself, is turned over, and that which was the upper side before is now pressed on a piece of felt between a pair of press rolls.

What is the next step in the process?

The sheet passes on to the drying cylinders.

How are they made?

These are hollow cast-iron rollers heated by steam forced into them.

How many are used at once?

The number varies in different mills, sometimes 20 are used.

Explain the method of drying.

The first cylinder is heated a very little ; in the second it is increased a few degrees, the third is still warmer, and thus the heat is gradually increased until we come to the last one, where it is the greatest of all.

Why are the sheets dried in this way?

It has been found that by so doing the paper is stronger and more durable than if only a few cylinders were taken.

What is now done with the paper?

It is either wound directly upon a reel, or first passed through several sets of calender rolls, that the surface may be smoothed and finished

How is the sizing applied for printing paper?

As we have already said, the glue and alum are mixed with the pulp.

Is the method the same for writing paper?

No ; the sizing for that is now usually applied to the web, by passing it through a solution of gelatine and alum, heated to about 100° F.

How is it dried?

This is done very quickly by running the web over several drums, the surface of which is pierced with holes,

Of what use are these openings?

By means of a revolving fan, a strong current of heated air is made to blow upon the sheet, which dries' it very rapidly.

Is the old method of drying on lines still in use?

Yes ; in some mills we find it practiced, and the paper thus prepared is much stronger than by the hot-air plan.

How large are the sheets thus made?

They are usually about 54 inches wide ; the machine running off 600 yards an hour, or a mile in three hours.

How are the sheets cut?

They are divided lengthwise by pairs of circular knives which revolve, one below and a larger one above the sheet, the movement being like that of a pair of scissors.

How are they cut across?

When the required length of paper is measured by the machine, two knives, one fixed, the other movable, also act like scissors upon the sheet

Explain how the paper is made to move along regularly.

A part of the machine, called the "*drum*," brings the sheet forward until it is of the right length, when it is held fast by two blocks, and the cutting takes place, the "drum" then returns for more paper and thus constantly works back and forth.

How is the glazing given to very fine writing paper?

This is done by placing polished sheets of copper between the paper and then rolling it. By repeating the operation several times the finish is greatly improved.

Are all the sheets found perfect when finished?

No; very many appear defective that seemed to be well made before passing through the glazing process.

What is done with them?

They are cast into the waste basket, and converted again into paper.

Can you mention any other uses, than those already mentioned, to which this article is applied?

We find that it answers many other purposes. Pasteboard, paper-boxes, paper-hangings, sheathing for vessels, carpets, the outer layer on the covers of books, etc., etc., are also made of it.

Can all of these articles be made by the Fourdrinier machine?

Yes; this machine is arranged, and the parts all connected, so that the whole process is carried on by it, from the pouring of the pulp into the vat, until the paper comes out at the other end complete and perfect.

SECTION V.

CHAPTER I.

PRINTING.

Does Printing rank among the ancient or modern arts ?

It may be classed among both.

Explain how this can be.

The simplest form of printing has been practiced by different nations from the earliest periods. But the wonderful improvements made in this art in latter ages may cause it to be regarded as a modern invention.

Will you mention some proofs that the ancients understood the art.

The bricks taken from the ruins of Egypt and Assyria are marked with characters formed in the clay. The Israelites used seals and signets—the Romans had stamps for marking the maker's or owner's name upon different articles, and also for branding cattle.

How may the idea of printing as we now understand it have been suggested to the inventors ?

The ruins of which we have spoken probably had

something to do with it, also the directions given by Cicero in one of his books regarding metal types, which he calls "forms of letters."

Before the invention of printing, as we now have it, how were records made ?

Entirely by writings, which of course required a great amount of time and labor.

What then are the principal advantages gained by this art ?

Books, papers, etc., have multiplied very rapidly, knowledge of all kinds is widely diffused, and thereby education becomes not only more general, but it is also very thorough, and of a higher order

When we read the history of ancient nations, what appears strange to us ?

As we discover the progress they had made in many of the arts and sciences, being even superior to us in some of them, it seems strange that they should have come so near the invention of movable types, and yet not have used them for so long a time.

What is probably the cause of this ?

It may be owing to the fact that they had no material, like our paper, which would receive the impression of the type.

When were these types first adopted?

Not until the 15th century.

Had other nations substituted any thing for this art?

Yes; the earliest records of the Chinese, Japanese and Tartars show that they were accustomed to print all their books from engraved blocks.

Do they still retain this method?

Yes; strange as it may seem, they do nearly all their printing in this way.

Can you give any reason for it.

Their love for old customs is so strong, that it is almost impossible to change them for others far better.

How do they regard themselves?

The people of Asia, particularly the Chinese, have so good an opinion of themselves, that they will hardly believe any other nation can excel their own, and this is another reason for not adopting modern inventions more readily.

Have they made much progress in the arts?

In some things they show even more skill than the Europeans.

For what are we indebted to them?

The manufacture of silk, China lacquered ware, etc., originated in China, and doubtless the idea of printing was suggested to Europeans, by seeing their modern block.

Are the Chinese still as reserved as ever?

Within a few years intercourse has been opened with China by means of treaties between that country and the U. S., by which there is more freedom of communication.

Have they adopted any of our inventions?

Yes ; to a limited extent. The Japanese seem to do so more readily than the Chinese. Our system of education is now being generally introduced into both Empires.

Will you explain their method of printing from blocks.

The first step in the process is to paste the page, which has been written on tracing paper, face downwards, upon a block of hard wood.

What does the engraver then do?

He cuts away the wood and paper not marked by lines, leaving the latter raised up, and the printer, with a fine brush dipped in ink blackens the whole surface.

How is the impression taken from this?

By laying upon the block a sheet of blank paper, and pressing it down with a soft dry brush.

How many pages can be printed at a time in this way?

Only two, having a line between them, by which the sheet is folded back to back. The open edges are bound together, while the closed one is in front.

Why are the leaves bound in this way?

Because only one side of the whole sheet is printed.

CHAPTER II.

THE MODERN METHOD OF PRINTING.

To whom are we indebted for this great invention ?

As often happens in similar cases many persons claim the honor. The City of Haarlem, in Holland, affirm that Laurens Janzoon Coster invented the art of printing in 1423 by using movable types of wood and afterwards of lead and tin.

Can any certain proofs of this be given ?

No ; as printed works by him cannot be produced.

Why is it difficult to settle this question satisfactorily ?

Because the invention of printing, like many others, was not wholly accomplished by one man.

How was it done ?

Various experiments were made by different persons, neither of which was completely successful, but all prepared the way, more or less, for the fortunate result.

HOE PRINTING PRESS

What person is now generally believed to have aided most in the work, so as to be called the inventor of printing ?

This great honor doubtless belongs to Johannes, or John Gutenberg.

What can you say of his efforts ?

He commenced by making experiments at Strasbourg, but kept the secret very carefully, until 1438, when it became known that he had made a printing press and movable types.

Did he produce any books ?

Not then. But in 1450 he returned to his native city, Mentz, where he had as partner Johann Faust, a wealthy gentleman, who agreed to furnish funds for carrying on the business in return for the secrets Gutenberg revealed to him.

Who became their assistant ?

Peter Schäffer, who had been employed for a long time in copying books.

Was he fitted for the work ?

Yes; they could hardly have found one more so. He substituted metal types, cast in plaster moulds, for those before made by Gutenberg, which were carved out of wood or metal. Other improvements were also made by him.

What success had these inventors ?

They printed several books. The first, bearing any date, was in 1455, being the letters of Pope Nicholas V.

What occurred soon after to check the work ?

The city of Mentz was besieged and captured by

Count Adolphus of Nassau, in 1462, when the printers were obliged to leave the country.

Was not this a great misfortune?

So it seemed at first, but the result proved it to be the best thing that could have happened.

Explain the reason.

The printers were scattered in different places, and practised their business in the new homes they had found. The art of course was more widely known, spread very rapidly, and soon became an important branch of trade.

Mention some of the places where it was introduced?

We find it at Subigeo, near Rome, in 1462 ; the types used there were more like the Roman form of letters, the Germans having imitated handwriting or adopted the Gothic form in their types.

Can you remember any other cities ?

The art was also practiced in Milan and Venice, in 1469, where the printers seemed particularly to excel.

Was any ornament then used in printing?

Yes ; a great deal. Some of the designs were so beautiful, that the books were often purchased as much for the pictures with which they were ornamented, as for the reading matter contained therein.

Was the value of the books always the same ?

No ; as years passed on, the oldest editions were always in demand.

What is the highest price ever paid for a book?

The greatest price given for a printed work was £2,260 or over $11,000 The book was a collection of stories by an Italian author written in 1571. This fabulous sum was paid by the Marquis of Blandford in 1812.

What progress did the art of printing make ?

It was introduced into Paris in 1470, into London in 1474, and before the year 1500, less than 50 years after its invention, printing presses were in operation in 220 different cities of Europe.

When was the first one used in our own country ?

The first printing press was introduced at Cambridge, Mass., in 1639.

What can you say of those then used ?

They were of course very simple in form, printing only four pages at a time, little improvement being made until the 17th century.

What kind of ink was used ?

At first the ink was made of brown umber, ground very fine and diluted.

Why was it preferred to the black ?

It seemed to harmonize better with the various colors used to ornament each page, although the printers sometimes used both black and red. These colors were so deep and rich, that time does not seem to have affected them in the least.

How did the first printing compare with that which is now executed ?

It was of course very rude, and sometimes quite difficult to read.

What was the cause of this ?

The words would often run together, as the spaces

were not regularly marked ; the punctuation was not correct, and abbreviations were often used.

How were the capitals made?

Spaces were left for these, which were afterwards filled in with fancy letters by those who were skillful in the work, as the printers were not able to imitate them in type.

What kind of ornaments were added?

There was a great variety in them, the wide margin of the pages being filled with figures of saints, flowers, birds, animals, monsters, etc.

Did these relate to the subject of the book?

Very often they had nothing at all to do with it, being used merely for ornament. The date and name of the printer seldom appeared ; if found at all they were at the end of the book.

When were the first decided improvements made in the art of printing?

About the year 1750, John Baskerville, of Birmingham, in England, by means of punches, produced a far better kind of type, so that the only changes since then have been to vary the forms of the letters, as well as the shading of the lines.

Where do we find the greatest variety frequently used?

It is often seen in advertisements, handbills, circulars, etc. Some of the styles show great taste and skill on the part of the type-maker.

Does the printer manufacture his own type?

This was formerly the custom, but for more than

200 years it has become a separate branch of the business.

Will you mention the names of the different sizes of type now used?

The Great Primer is the largest, except for handbills. Then follow in order of size

English   Pica,   Small Pica,

Long Primer,   Bourgeois,   Brevier,

Minion,   Nonpareil,   Agate.,

Pearl,   Diamond.,

the last being the smallest as will be seen by the specimens given above.

What is a font or fount?

It is a complete assortment of letters of one size, a certain number of each being necessary. For example, there must be three complete alphabets in Capitals, small capitals, and small or "lower case" letters as they are called, also the ff either united to, or separate from *i* and *l* : diphthongs, figures, punctuation marks, the signs used for contractions, as &, $, £, etc., besides references and other marks each one of which requires a separate piece of type.

What are used to regulate the distances between words?

Those not separated by punctuation marks, require a square piece of plain metal as large as one of the small letters. One of these is placed between each word, as will be soon explained.

Is any thing else necessary to make a complete "font"?

Other forms of types are used for certain kinds of books, as those which treat of astronomy, mathematics, etc., but for general purposes, the above are sufficient.

What does the following table show?

It gives the usual number of each of the small letters with the more common punctuation marks found in a "*font.*"

a—	8,500	q—	500
e—12,000		r—	6,200
i—	8,000	s—	8,000
o—	8,000	t—	9,000
u—	3,400	v—	1,200
b—	1,600	w—	2,000
c—	3,000	x—	400
d—	4,400 •	y—	2,000
f—	2,517	z—	200
g—	1,700		4,500
h—	6,400		800
j—	400		600
k—	800		2,000
l—	4,000	Thick spaces	18,000
m—	3,000	Middle "	12,000
n—	8,000	Thin "	8,000
p—	1,750	Hair "	3,000

CHAPTER III.

PROCESS OF PRINTING EXPLAINED.

How are the letters in a "font" arranged?

For the convenience of the printer, the letters of one kind are placed in separate boxes or cells of two open cases arranged in a slanting position one above the other, so as to be more easily reached. The upper case contains the large and small capitals, with references, dashes, etc.

What are kept in the lower case?

In this are found type of different sizes, adapted for any purpose required. The spaces, points, figures, etc., are also in this case.

Has any improvement been made upon the above plan?

Yes ; Mr. Thomas N. Rooker of New York has so arranged the type that one case can be used instead of two. There is still another method invented by him, in which the boxes have movable bottoms, tha can be raised or lowered by a screw.

What is the advantage of this?

The type-setter, or "*compositor,*" as he is called, can

thus have the letters nearer at hand, and is therefore able to do much more work in the same time.

Having the boxes before him, how does the compositor work ?

The copy or manuscript is laid before him ; he takes in his left hand the composing-stick, as it is called, which is a little iron tray large enough to hold about ten lines, the exact length of each line being regulated by a slide at the side.

What is then done ?

He sets the first type in the left hand corner of the " stick," face downward, the form of the letter being reversed, so that the impression may be correct ; the remaining letters follow very quickly, and at the end of each word a " space " is set.

When the printer comes to the end of the line, does he leave it ?

No ; he re-arranges the words and spaces so there shall be equal distances between them. Much skill is required to do this well and quickly. He then proceeds in the same way with the remaining lines.

When all are finished, what follows ?

The compositor slips off the type thus arranged upon a larger tray called a "galley."

Is this easily done ?

No ; great care is necessary that the pieces may not fall out of place, or as the printers call it, "be thrown into pi."

When the "galleys" are filled, what is done?

It is from these that the pages are formed. The

bottom of the first one is marked with "A" or "1" to indicate the first page—upon the 9th or 17th "B" or "2" is stamped. This is done for the convenience of the binder, who can then more readily gather and fold the sheets.

What is done with the pages when formed?

The type for each of them is bound with twine and then set in order for printing upon an iron or marble block, called the "imposing stone."

Upon what do the form of the pages depend?

They depend upon the size of the book to be made. These different sizes have received different names. When the sheet is folded so as to form four leaves, it is called a folio—if eight, a quarto—sixteen, an octavo—24, a duodecimo, etc.

Were these terms always used?

The names have not changed, but before the use of steam in printing, they indicated half the numbers which they now do. As 2 leaves for a folio, 4 for a quarto, etc.

Are the pages arranged in the order for reading them?

No ; they are placed so that only one side of a sheet shall be printed from them, and when folded 4, 8, or 12 times, will then come in regular order.

How can you show this?

By taking a double newspaper of 8 pages and spreading it out. On one side are the 1st, 8th, 4th, and 5th pages, and on the other the 2d, 3d, 6th, and 7th.

When the pages are properly arranged what is then done?

A "first proof" as it is called, that is, a copy is struck off by laying a sheet of blank paper on the types thus arranged, which is pressed down by a hand roller.

Why is only one copy taken at first?

This is the one to be examined by the proof-reader, who marks the errors by certain signs. The compositor then corrects them by changing the type.

Are any other "proofs" taken?

Yes; after the first correction, more copies are struck off to be corrected by the author, or "proof-readers" again.

What then follows?

The final corrections being made, the prepared pages of type are taken to the printing-press, which is worked by steam, and by means of this wonderful machine, 15,000 impressions of a newspaper are struck off in an hour.

Is steam now used for all kinds of printing?

No ; a hand-press is employed in offices where very fine, nice work is to be done—or when but few copies of an article are required.

When was steam first used for printing?

On the 28th Nov., 1814, the London Times issued the first sheet ever printed by steam.

CHAPTER IV.

STEREOTYPE PRINTING.

When the required number of copies of a book or newspaper are struck off, what is done with the type?

It is divided again among the different boxes from which it was taken.

If more copies of the same book are required how are they obtained?

The type must be set again as at first.

Is there any other method?

Yes; by an ingenious contrivance, additional impressions can be taken at any time.

How was this done at first?

In the early part of the 18th century Van der May, of Leyden, in Holland, made the types, after they were set for printing, into a solid plate, by soldering the lower ends together.

Did this answer the required purpose?

Yes; very well for the particular book or paper to be printed, but the type could not be used for other work.

What was the next improvement ?

William Ged of Edinburgh invented a method by which the work could be *stereotyped,* as it is called, and the same type used again for other purposes.

Did he accomplish much by this invention ?

He met with so much opposition from the type founders, or those who had made the type, as it of course lessened their business, that he was obliged to give up his plan after using it a short time.

Was another attempt made ?

Nearly 70 years afterwards, Didot, a Frenchman following up the idea of Ged, made the type of harder metal than usual, by the addition of copper.

What was done with it ?

The page being properly formed from this type, an impression of it was taken on a smooth sheet of soft lead : this could be put away for future use.

Were copies struck from this sheet?

No ; but impressions could be taken from it, upon a sheet of type metal, when the latter was so hot as to be soft, and from this copies could be struck off at any time, while the loose types from which the impression was taken in lead, could be "*set up*" again for other books or papers.

What can you say of this method of stereotyping ?

It answered the purpose very well, but a still better plan is now adopted called the paper process.

Will you explain it ?

The type is prepared as usual for one page. A sheet of paper is then laid upon the table and brushed over with a solution of gum, a sheet of tissue paper is added, then more gum, and so on until a moulding sheet about $\frac{1}{32}$ of an inch in thickness is formed.

What follows ?

The "*form*" of type as the page is called, is laid upon an iron table and slightly oiled on the upper side. The moulding sheet is placed on this and beaten down with a stiff brush by which it receives an impression from the "*form*"

Is the process now finished ?

No; woollen cloths are thrown over it, and the whole put on a steam table, and under a "*platen*."

What is a platen ?

This name is applied by printers to the flat part of the press which is screwed down on the moulding sheet.

After remaining under press for some time what is the result?

When taken out, a perfect impression of the type is found on the matrix or moulding sheet, which is as firm and pliable as bristol-board.

What is then done with it ?

The matrix, now stamped from the type, is placed in a mould made of iron covered very closely and then set on end; a mixture of different metals being melted, is poured over the matrix through an opening at the top.

Why is this done ?

As the metal cools a complete covering is thus formed, which receives a perfect impression from the stamped sheet; it is removed from the matrix as soon as possible, cooled still more and hardened in cold water.

What is this sheet of metal called?

It is called the stereotype plate.   At least 200,000 copies can be taken from it at any time when required.

Does it require much time to prepare the stereotype plates?

Very little is necessary.   The average time for stereotyping double sheet newspapers is 30 to 35 minutes, although it can be done in 20 minutes.

Is this method now adopted to any extent?

Yes ; nearly every book, and the most popular newspapers are stereotyped, or "*cast*" as it is called.

SECTION VI.

CHAPTER I.

COTTON MANUFACTURERS.

How is Cotton obtained?

It is taken from a plant growing in warm countries in various parts of the world.

Are there any varieties in the shrub?

There are three principal kinds, viz.: the herbaceous or annual, the shrub that lives two or three years, and the tree which lasts twenty years.

Are these all cultivated in the United States?

No; the annual is the only one raised here.

In what part of the country is it found?

It is principally cultivated in the extreme south, as the soil and climate seem better adapted to it.

Has it ever been raised farther north?

Yes; at first small portions of land from New Jersey to Georgia might be seen covered with cotton plants. Each family cultivated what was necessary for its own use.

Is there more than one kind of the annual plant?

Yes ; there are three varieties ; the Sea-island cotton, the medium, and the short staple.

Which is the most valuable?

The Sea-island is the best, on account of the long,
fine, silky threads drawn from it.

Where is it raised?

The greatest quantities are found around the islands
south of the United States, and on the lands that
border on the Gulf of Mexico.   It is also raised on
the Florida coast, as well as through the State.

Is it all equally good?

No ; that upon the more elevated parts is inferior
in quality and quantity.

*Is the Sea-island cotton produced in other parts of
the world?*

The soil and climate of the United States seem
better adapted for this variety than any other country.
For although in Egypt, the Isle of Bourbon and Per-
nambuco, the best cottons are raised, yet even there the
Sea-island does not equal ours in the length and fine-
ness of the thread.

*How does this variety compare in value with the
Short Staple?*

It is considered worth two, three and even four
times as much as any other, being sometimes sold for
$1.00 per pound.

*What kind is ranked next in value to the Sea-
island?*

The Egyptian and Brazilian, being used for fine

fabrics. The "Medium Staple" produced here comes next, common yarn and coarse cloth being made from it.

Which is the lowest in value?

That from India is the coarsest, not being white and clean. It is mixed with the American variety and used for the most common cloth.

If there was enough Sea-island cotton, could we dispense with the other varieties?

No ; each particular kind seems equally necessary for the different uses made of it. The medium-staple is raised in the greatest quantities, there being more general uses to which it can be applied.

When does the planting of cotton-seed take place?

In the United States, the ground is ploughed in February, and the seed planted from the 15th of March to the 1st of April, according to the latitude of the place.

When the plants first appear, what is done?

The weakest and smallest are cut down, leaving the others in bunches. In a few days these are again thinned out, when only two stalks are left, and finally but one remains.

What is done to the land during this time?

It is constantly broken up with hoes and ploughs.

When does this plant begin to ripen?

In the month of July. The cotton is formed in pods ; when these burst open, the white downy lint appears.

Is the cotton all picked at once?

No; at first but few of the pods are open, yet as soon as the cotton appears on any of the plants, the men, women, and children pass between the rows, gathering from each side as they go.

When is the busiest time?

In September—then the fields are white as if covered with snow. It is necessary to gather as quickly as possible, lest the rain may beat down and scatter the precious crop.

How long does the picking season last?

It usually continues from July until Christmas.

What may be seen during all this time?

Troops of men, women, and children passing between the rows, each wearing a bag around the neck to hold the cotton. When this is full it is emptied into baskets at the end of the rows.

How often do the laborers go through the fields?

It is necessary to go over them five or six times, as the plants ripen so gradually.

What is done with the cotton when gathered?

Sometimes it is carried directly to the packing-house, but is generally spread on scaffolds to dry, and to be cleaned of any trash that may have fallen into it.

How much can each person pick in a day?

A good laborer will gather from 250 to 300 pounds per day—although some are able to do even more.

When the cotton has been dried, what is done with it?

It is taken to the packing-house, where it is ginned,

weighed, packed and delivered to the nearest railway station.

How is it ginned?

The seed is separated from the lint by a very wonderful machine invented by Mr. Whitney, an American.

CHAPTER II.

PROGRESS OF THE MANUFACTURE IN DIFFERENT COUNTRIES.

How long has cotton been used as material for clothing?

This is not certainly known. But we find in the earliest records, mention made of it not only in the civilized parts of the world, but also among rude and savage people.

Where was the cotton obtained that is used in the United States?

It is a native of Mexico, the people of that country made nearly all their clothing from that material, as they had neither hemp, wool, or silk.

How did the Mexicans use the cotton?

They wove large webs as delicate as any now made, and embroidered upon them figures of animals and flowers, by means of furs and feathers.

When Cortez invaded Mexico how did he dispose of some of these garments?

They were considered so beautiful that he sent a few of the richest to King Charles V. of Spain.

Was the art of manufacturing cotton then made known?

No; it seems to have been lost at the time, as the Spaniards were fighting with the Mexicans, but the plant was introduced into this country when our government was formed.

What can you say of the cotton culture here?

It can be raised in such large quantities, and with so little expense, that we are able to furnish it to the Europeans much cheaper than they can obtain it elsewhere.

How has the crop increased?

In 1800 there were raised in the United States, 9,532,263 lbs. of cotton, which, when manufactured, sold for 48 cts. per yd.   In 1859, the crop amounted to 2,162,000,000 lbs. at 6 cts. per yd., since then there has been a constant increase in the business.

To what has this rapid progress been owing?

It results chiefly from the wonderful inventions that have been made, not only in manufacturing the goods, but in preparing the raw material for use.

Have machines always been employed?

By no means.   Although cotton goods have been manufactured in India from the earliest ages, yet the work was almost entirely done by hand, the few machines being very rude and imperfect.

What can you say of the cloth produced there?

It is more delicate than any other, being so fine that when laid on the grass and covered with dew it cannot be seen.

Is it easily done?

No; the process is very slow and tedious; four months are required to make one piece, which is then worth 500 Rupees or about $250.

Is this peculiar kind of cloth made in all parts of India?

No; each district produces a different web. Long training, and much patience are necessary to understand the business.

In what other countries was cotton manufactured?

In the 11th century it passed from India to China, and afterwards over to Europe, although it did not make much progress until the 17th century.

Did the ancient Egyptians understand the art?

It was supposed for a long time that they did, as the mummy cloths were believed to have been made of cotton, but on close examination of the threads, they are found to be of flax.

What is the difference between a thread of cotton and one of flax?

The former is flat and twisted, while the latter is round and jointed.

Did the manufacture of cotton make much progress in Great Britain?

No; very little. This was owing to want of material and good machines.

When did a change for the better take place?

About the time of the Revolutionary War. Many inventions and improvements were then made, by which more and better goods were produced with far less time and labor.

Will you mention the different steps in the process of manufacture ?

After gathering the cotton, it passes through the " Gin," a machine which separates the lint from the seed. It is then cleaned, carded, spun, wove, dyed and printed.

Why is it necessary to card the cotton ?

That it may be drawn out into straight threads, to be spun and woven.

How was this formerly done ?

Two flat " cards," resembling curry-combs, were held in the hand, the cotton being carefully combed through them as straight as possible—the roll that came out was called a " *Sliver*," which was twisted on a wheel near by into a thick thread, like candlewick ; this was the " *roving*."

What was then done with it ?

The roving being again twisted, was spun into a single thread, and in this way all the cotton yarn of the country was slowly made by females at their own homes.

How was the weaving done ?

The simple looms used were worked also by hand.

When did a change for the better first take place ?

In 1767, when James Hargreaves used a wheel that would drive eight spindles at once, the " *rovings*" being drawn through a clasp held in the left hand.

What followed ?

Two years later Mr. Arkwright added rollers or drawing frames, which was a great improvement.

Explain in what way.

The "roving" on its way, passed between two rollers, and from these to another pair, moving twice as fast as the first.

What was the result?

The rolls of cotton were drawn out to twice their former length and half the thickness. This was done in a shorter time and much more evenly than before.

What name did Mr. Arkwright give his machine?

He called it his "Spinning-Jenny"—being named, as some say, from his wife, Jennie Arkwright.

What improvement followed?

In 1784 Mr. Crompton produced a third machine, using the plan found in the previous ones. Before this the spindles could not be moved. Now they were fixed upon a frame which would run out 56 inches, stretch and twist the thread, and returning wind it upon the spindles, making it much finer, stronger and more even than before.

How many spindles could be used on this machine?

It would carry 130, and when water-power was applied, 400. Now the machine is self-acting, 300 is the usual number.

What can you say of the improvements in the remaining steps of the business.

They are all as great, as these. The rudest machines at first used, have given place to the beautiful, swift, noiseless ones now found throughout our country.

CHAPTER III.

METHOD OF MANUFACTURE.

What has been one great cause of the improvements in manufacturing goods ?

The use of steam, where water power could not be obtained; and even where the latter may be had, some think the former better and cheaper.

We have already described the growth, picking and packing of cotton ; will you now tell me the next step in the process ?

When the bales are brought to the mill, the contents of one is spread out upon the floor, upon this another is scattered, and so on until a huge pile called a " *bing* " is raised.

What is then done ?

A rake is used to scrape down the sides, thus thoroughly mixing all together, as the qualities in each bale of the same staple being different, should be combined.

What do you mean by " staple ? "

As we have already said, the term is applied to the three different kinds of cotten raised, viz. : long, medium, and short staple, according to the length of the natural fibre.

For what is the " long staple" required ?

It is used for the threads that run lengthwise of the cloth, as no other kind will answer the purpose.

Of what are the cross threads made ?

The "medium staple" answers for this, which is called the "weft," the other being the warp. It is softer and more silky than the long staple and fills up better.

What use is made of the short staple?

It is sometimes taken for the " weft," but it is not so smooth as the other kinds, being more like wool; if much of it is used, the cloth becomes thin and flimsy after washing and bleaching, so that it is better to mix a little with the " medium."

When the cotton is mixed is it perfectly clean ?

No, very far from being so ; therefore it is necessary to cleanse it.

How is this done ?

Various machines are used, the best seems to be the one called " the Willey."

How does it work ?

There are two large iron wheels, each having four stout teeth ; these are placed face to face so that the teeth will clash against each other. The cotton passing between them, when the machine is in motion, is torn apart.

What becomes of the impurities?

A revolving fan attached to the machine, blows the

dirt through a tube attached to it, leaving the cotton white and fleecy.

How fast do these wheels revolve ?

About 1600 times in a minute.

What becomes of the cotton ?

It passes out of the " Willey " into a second machine, called the "spreader," where it is acted upon by blunt knives that clean it still more.

How does it then look ?

As it comes from this machine it is in the form of a thin sheet ; being wound upon a roller it is necessary to have this sheet very even ; if there are thin and thick places, they will afterwards appear in the cloth.

What is done with these sheets ?

They are now carded, that is, combed out; the cotton being straightened into a delicate fleece. It is then drawn through a funnel, coming out in long close rolls, looking like a stream of cream as they pass into tin cans prepared for them.

Is this carding repeated ?

For very fine yarn, finer cards are afterwards used.

What follows ?

The work has thus far been done by males ; females now continue it, carrying the " *slivers,*" as the rolls are called, through the " drawing" process.

How is this done ?

By means of rollers ; the slivers coming from the tin cans being taken by one roller, and passing over to another the rolls are drawn out into thread. The end of one "sliver" being laid upon the middle of another makes them even; this is called "doubling," or drawing in and out.

How often is it repeated?

The more the better—sometimes the doubling is done 32,000 times for one thread.

Is it then very firm?

No; when it comes from the drawing frame it is very thin and delicate, and must be twisted once or twice, when it is ready for spinning, which is done by spindles that wind the yarn at the same time upon spools called "*bobbins*."

What is done with the bobbins?

When full, they are set in a frame so that the thread can be wound off upon a large six-sided reel.

What is the size of it?

The reel is $1\frac{1}{2}$ yds. in circumference; by revolving 560 times, one "hank" of yarn is wound; this is then tied, other "hanks" are added, and when taken off and weighed the number or quality of the yarn is known.

Explain this?

A hank of the coarsest yarn weighs half a pound; the common quality gives from 10 to 40 hanks in a pound. The finest runs up to 300 hanks per. pound, although at the World's Fair in London, some was ex-bited giving 600 hanks to the pound. A dress for the Queen was made of 460 thread.

How does this compare with the delicate India fabrics?

It far exceeds them; one specimen of spinning produced a thread 1,026 miles in length from a pound of cotton.

What are often attached to the spinning machines ?

Clocks are sometimes placed there, so arranged as to mark the quantity of work done in a week ; this is registered upon a board hung up in sight of all the operatives ; the monthly wages are paid according to the amount of work credited to each one.

Is the yarn ready for weaving as soon as it is spun ?

That for the filling or cross threads can be used ; but the warp or long threads must be " dressed " first, that is, a kind of sizing is applied making the yarn stiff and smooth, when it is taken to the weaving-room.

How many machines are found here ?

Sometimes 600 looms, attended by 150 girls.

What is done with the cloth after weaving ?

It is taken to another room to be trimmed, measured, folded, marked, and made into bales for the market, or sent to the Print shops to be made into calico.

CHAPTER IV.

GREATER IMPROVEMENTS.

Where were the first mills in the U.S. erected for the manufacture of cotton?

At Pawtucket; the first factory was built by Samuel Slater and two other gentlemen, where every variety of spinning was done.

What machines were used?

The machines were brought from England, and proved to be so excellent that they were constantly used for forty years.

What has become of the factory erected by Mr. Slater?

A few years ago it was still standing. Then there could be seen two of the spinning frames used in 1789, being kept as curiosities.

Were the English willing other nations should use their machines?

No; a law was passed forbidding any wool òr machines to be exported; this was in force until 1828.

What caused it to be withdrawn?

They found the Americans were becoming even more ingenious than themselves, and so thought it would be for their own advantage to be more liberal and friendly.

If such was the case, how did Mr. Slater obtain his machines ?

Although he was so closely watched by the English, that he could not even smuggle so much as a drawing or pattern of a machine, yet as he had gained a thorough *knowledge* of the spinning business before leaving England, he made good use of it now.

Explain in what way.

With his own hands, and by great ingenuity, he made three cards, and twenty-two spindles, which was the beginning of the great manufacturing business in this country.

What results have followed this first attempt ?

Our rivers and water-falls propel thousands of mill-wheels, and millions of shuttles and spindles, giving constant employment and an honorable support to a vast number of persons.

Was cloth also manufactured in Mr. Slater's mill ?

No ; his machines were only for the spinning of yarn or thread to be afterwards knit or woven into cloth.

How had the weaving been done before 1812?

The looms were worked altogether by hand, as persons even now weave rag-carpets.

Were any improvements made ?

Yes ; although the war of 1812 prevented all intercourse with Great Britain, which seemed to check the progress of manufacturers, yet the result proved otherwise.

How could this be ?

As we have before said regarding spinning machines, it was impossible to obtain a drawing or model
from England ; the case was similar as to looms, but
the very difficulty brought its own remedy.

In what way ?

Just as the war was about to break out, Mr. Francis
C. Lowell returned from Europe, where he had gained
much knowledge of the manufacturing business, hoping
to make many changes for the better in this country.

Did he succeed?

After many difficulties he accomplished the work.

How was it done ?

By the aid of his memory and skill alone ; in connection with Mr. Jackson, a power-loom was invented,
that is, one that would run by water-power.

Was it a perfect machine ?

By no means ; many defects were afterwards found
in it, yet it was so far a success, that the inventors
decided to erect a mill for weaving cotton cloth.

Was any thing besides weaving done here ?

This was the only intention at first, but as it was
found to be cheaper to make their own yarn than to
buy it, the owners decided to include in their establishment a mill for spinning.

How many spindles were used?

The mill, when finished in 1813, contained 1700
spindles.

Where was it built ?

At Waltham, Mass., where it is still in operation.

What was there remarkable about it?

At the time of its erection, it was *the only one in the world* where all the operations took place of converting the raw cotton into finished cloth.

With all the success thus gained what difficulty presented itself?

It was not an easy matter to obtain operatives.

Why was this so?

In England the people are so graded that there is always a poorer class where such operatives are easily found; but in America, we being "all free and equal," there is of course no such distinction here.

How was the difficulty remedied?

Boarding-houses were erected for the use of the factory people alone. Persons of excellent character were placed at the head of them to keep order, and to see that all the inmates were respectable and well behaved.

What resulted from this plan?

Parents were not afraid to place their daughters in these establishments. In a few years they had acquired money sufficient for a marriage portion, or to support themselves without labor, and when they left the mill, there were always enough to fill their places.

What resulted from the success of the first mill?

Others were soon established elsewhere.

Which were the principal of these?

That at Lowell, Mass.

To what was its success chiefly owing?

9

At the time of the war of 1812 considerable cotton had accumulated at the South making it very cheap. Commerce was also interrupted, so that the people turned their attention more to manufacturing than any thing else.

Did each factory in the country perform all the operations for making cloth?

No; this was chiefly the case in the N. E. mills, those in the Middle States being principally for spinning.

What progress did the Lowell mills make in their business?

In 1831, ten years after beginning, 530,461,990 yds. of cloth were made, or about twenty yards for each person in the country.

In which State is the business carried on most extensively?

In Mass., where it commenced. The money there invested is about one third of all the capital thus used in the U. S. The products are nearly in the same proportion.

CHAPTER V.

CALICO PRINTING.

How is cotton bleached?

Formerly, six or eight months were required for the cloth to steep in strong lye, and then bleach upon the grass.

What is the method now?

A bleaching powder composed of lime, salt, sulphuric acid, and manganese is used that will change the rough, dirty cloth as it comes from the weaver into the smooth, white fabric called bleached cotton.

Is any thing done to the cloth before bleaching?

Yes ; as it comes from the factory it is often soiled and greasy, so that it must be thoroughly cleansed.

How is this done?

The cloth is put into tubs, large enough to hold 500 pieces, where it is steeped for some hours in warm water, then washed in the dash-wheel.

What is the dash-wheel?

It is a machine similar to the one used in private families for washing, of course being much larger.

What?follows ?

The cloth is boiled in a preparation of lime-water, washed again as before, boiled in alkali, washed once more, steeped in bleaching-powder some hours, then in oil of vitriol and water, washed for the last time in the dash-wheel, squeezed between rollers, mangled and dried in the air or in warm rooms.

Why is it necessary to go through all this process ?

Because if the cloth is not perfectly clear and white, it will be impossible to have a good and brilliant color formed, with a distinct ground.

How long a time is required for this process ?

Only a few hours.

Why is Calico so called ?

The name is said to be derived from Calicut, a town on the Malabar coast, whence it was first imported.

How is the term used ?

In England, the white, unprinted cloth is called calico, but with us the term is adapted to pieces of cotton stamped with various colored figures.

How long has stamped cloth been used ?

Probably for many centuries ; Homer and Herodotus both mention the rich, linen goods ornamented with figures of birds, etc., dyed in fast colors.

When did these writers live ?

They were both Greeks ; Homer, the poet, lived 915 B.C., and Herodotus, the historian, 445 B.C.

Does any other author give similar accounts ?

Yes ; Pliny, a famous Roman author, relates the method used by the Egyptians in coloring their cloth.

Will you explain it?

He says the Egyptians take white cloth, and having drawn the figures they wish, apply certain kinds of drugs to these places.

Does the colored pattern then appear?

No ; the cloth still looks perfectly white. But having been put in a kettle of some coloring liquid, scalding hot, the figures appear very brilliant and beautiful, and the very colors themselves are perfectly "*fast.*"

What is the strangest part of the process ?

The most wonderful thing connected with it is, that one simple coloring liquid should bring out so many different shades at the same time.

Can you mention any other nations that understand the art of printing calico ?

In India, much skill is shown by the natives who practice the art. The Chinese also produce a kind of chintz counter-pane, with the strange figures so peculiar to them.

How is it done ?

The pattern being drawn is covered with wax, and the parts not thus protected will be colored when dipped in the dye-kettle.

What progress did the art make ?

It proceeded very slowly ; although introduced from India into England it was not until some time in the 17th century that the business began to flourish

In what city ?

In Augsburg, Bavaria, where the printed cotton and linen goods were quite famous.

In what other countries did it then find its way ?

Into France, Germany, Switzerland and Great Britain. It first appeared in London in 1676.

Did it progress rapidly in London ?

No, very slowly ; meeting with great opposition from the silk and woollen weaver, whose trade was injured by it.

What law was passed to prevent the sale of calico ?

In 1720 a law was passed, forbidding anyone to wear it under a penalty of £5, the seller being fined £20.

How long did this continue ?

It was not until 1831 that the heavy fines and taxes were removed. Since then the business has been very flourishing.

How was calico printed at first?

It was done by means of wooden blocks ; one of a few inches square was pressed upon the cloth by hand, leaving a single color. As other figures and colors were of course required for the pattern, a separate block was used for each one.

What can you say of this process ?

It was very slow and tedious.

What improvement was soon made in this method?

Immense machines were invented, in which the blocks were so arranged that 15 or 20 colors could be printed at once, and so rapidly that 600 or 700 times as many pieces were produced as before in a single day, at the rate of a mile an hour.

Are the patterns drawn by the calico printer?

No; this is a separate part of the business, and is done by artists called designers.

Explain how they form the patterns?

It depends almost entirely upon their own skill and ingenuity. They are first taught in "Schools of Design."

How are the lessons given?

The pupil is first required to make straight and curved lines readily and accurately; then to form as many different figures as possible out of a certain number of straight or curved lines, afterwards to use both at once.

What is the next step?

After succeeding well in that part of the instruction, he is required to apply colors to these various figures in as many ways as possible. The pupil is now ready to be a designer himself.

Is it a profitable business?

Yes, for a skillful artist. Manufacturers often pay $4000 per year for patterns.

Where are the most skillful designers found?

The French have thus far produced the most beautiful patterns. The best artists, however, are those who can have great variety as well as beauty in their designs.

Why is this necessary?

Because the taste of persons differ so much. A rude Indian is more pleased with large, showy figures than with small, delicate ones. Besides, our taste is such that we always require something new.

If cotton cloth is to be printed, what is necessary ?

It must be "*calendered*," as it is called.

What is meant by that term ?

Cloth to be " calendered " must pass between heated iron cylinders that are constantly turning; but before this the cotton must be "*singed.*"

Explain the process ?

The cloth is drawn quickly over a gas pipe having many little openings; the long line of flame singes the loose threads and soft down.   Another pipe above, exhausted of air, draws the flame through the goods.

Does it not burn the cloth ?

No ; as it moves very quickly, about three feet in a second, the loose threads are only burned ; the cloth, however, turns yellow, but it can be bleached in a few hours.

When this process is finished what follows ?

The cloth is now ready to be printed, which, as we have said, was formerly done by blocks ; they are also used now to some extent.

What other method is adopted ?

Copper cylinders are used upon which the pattern is cut.   There is one for each color to be applied.

How is the cylinder worked ?

By means of machinery it continually revolves, leaving the impression of the colored figure required, then other cylinders follow with whatever color is to be used ; in this way the printing is quickly done.

What is necessary in regard to the colors used?

Great care is taken that they are not too thin or too thick, so they may not spread or run into each other.

How is the color put upon the roller?

There is another cylinder below the one on which the pattern is engraved, this dips into a trough while revolving, taking as much of the dye as is necessary, which it rubs upon the upper roller, both turning together.

Will it not cover the whole of the roller?

Yes, it might, but there is a sharp blade of steel scraping all the time against the upper cylinder, which takes off all the color, except that in the parts cut out for the pattern.

What may be said of this machine?

It is certainly one of the most wonderful ever invented.

Is the color formed by each roller, the one that will appear when the cloth is finished?

No; that is merely the "sightening," as it is called, or a color by which the workman may judge of the correctness of the work thus far: this color is temporarily given by the mordant.

What is the "mordant?"

It is the peculiar substance which, being applied to the cotton on the printed figure, will dye it *there*, but nowhere else, although the whole piece of cloth may afterwards be dipped in the dye-kettle. The word is from the Latin "mordere," "to bite," as the color seems to bite, or fix itself in the cloth.

What are the " mordants " generally used?

Alum and copperas ; each of which is first changed to "iron-liquor," as it is called, by taking away the oil of vitriol from both, and substituting vinegar instead.

How are the different colors for dyeing prepared?

By adding madder to the iron-liquor, black and purple can be obtained, alum will dye red of different shades, and by using the two dyes chocolate appears.

By applying these different " mordants" to the calico what follows?

Although sixteen pieces may be put in the same coloring vat at once, yet each will come out with its own peculiar shade, according to the mordant used. It was probably on this principle that the ancients, to whom we have referred, produced their colored fabrics.

Can the cloth be put into the dye-kettles as soon as the " mordant" is applied?

No ; two or three weeks are required for it to become "fixed" sufficiently, if left untouched, but by the use of different substances the color can be "set" in two or three days when it is dyed. It is then rinsed, washed at the dash-wheel, passed through hot bran water, two or three times, and last through soda and water, when being again washed, is dried and ready to be folded.

What is done with the calico as soon as printed?

It is at once drawn over rollers in a room heated to 200°, that it may be thoroughly dried and the colors made "fast."

SECTION VII.

CHAPTER I.

WOOLLEN MANUFACTURES.

Has wool been used for a long time in making cloth?

Yes; it was probably the first material applied to such a purpose.

Why do we think so?

The history of nations confirms the belief, and as the first clothing was merely the skins of wild beasts, it was natural to suppose the hair and fur of animals would be the first material used for the purpose.

How was the cloth made for a long time?

As all the machines were very rude and simple, being worked by hand, the process was very slow and tedious.

Were improvements made?

Yes; by degrees. All that we have said regarding the progress of cotton manufactures will apply to woollen;

the machines used, and the method followed, being
also similar.

When the yarn is spun, what is done with it?

It is wound like the cotton upon a reel, which
however is only a yard in circumference. When this
has revolved 80 times it rings a bell and is then
stopped when the "ley," as it is called, is tied and the
reel revolves as before.

How many " leys" make a hank?

Seven, equal to 560 yds. Each hank being weighed,
as is done with cotton, will give the number of the yarn.
"No. 24" means that 24 hanks make a pound of that
quality.

*Are any materials except wool used in the manu-
facture of woollen goods?*

Yes; in nearly all kinds of cloth; for in the best,
as cassimeres, broadcloths, etc., though the warp and
woof are partly of wool, yet cotton and other materials
are often combined with it.

After the cloth is woven what is done with it?

The pieces are taken to a mill to be "fulled," that
is, scoured, cleansed and shrunk so as to be more firm
and durable.

*How much time is required to "full" a piece of
cloth?*

For broadcloth usually from 60 to 65 hours are
necessary—about 11 lbs. of soap being used. In
this process it will shrink in length from 54 to 40
yds., and in width from 12 to 7 quarters, or from 3
yds. to 1¾.

When "fulled," what is done with the cloth?

It is stretched on tenter-frames to dry in the open air, any defects then found are remedied.

How is the "nap" formed?

This is a delicate operation, lest the cloth should be injured. Sometimes it is done by scratching the goods with "combs" or teasing cards made of wire, or with the teasle plant.

What is this plant?

It belongs to the thistle class, producing burrs with very sharp, stiff points

Is there any other method?

Yes ; in large mills, the "gig-machine" is used, which is a cylinder covered with teasles, and made to revolve very rapidly as the cloth passes over it.

How are the goods colored?

For those to be printed, as in De Laines, the process is the same as described for calicoes, the mordant colored threads are dyed before weaving.

How are they used to form the pattern?

Each color for its particular part of the figure is woven so as to appear on the surface, the others are only seen on the under side, in that place, but are brought out in turn when required.

Has the progress of woollen manufactures been as great in this country as that of other goods?

The improvements are equally great, but in the quantity of goods produced, cotton takes the lead.

How in regard to the quality of wool?

Within the past few years, farmers have turned

their attention so much to the raising of sheep, secur
ing the finest breeds, that the wool brought to the
market equals, if not excels, that of any other country.

Does the supply equal the demand?

No ; it has been found necessary to import at
least one-third of all that is used here.

What is the quality of that imported?

It is usually of a coarser description, intended for
carpets, etc. That from S. America is very fine, but
so filled with the burr of a plant peculiar to the coun
try as to make it of little value.

CHAPTER II.

CARPETS.

Have carpets always been used ?

In Egypt and the Asiatic countries, the art of making very beautiful carpets has long been known, but it was some time before the Europeans used them.

What were substituted ?

Rushes, hay, straw, etc. ; even in the time of Queen Mary, rushes were strewn on the floor of her presence chamber.

Are carpets now used as much in Europe as in America ?

No ; the people of our own country seem to have a special fancy for them, every hall and room in their houses, the floors of the poorest churches, and even the counting-rooms of the merchants must be carpeted.

How is it in other countries ?

They are wanting in a thousand places where we use them, and as we do not manufacture enough for home consumption, at least 2,000,000 yds. are imported yearly.

What varieties can you mention?

The most common, made in families, is the rag-carpet; then follow ingrain, three-ply, Venetian, tapestries, Brussels, velvet and Wilton.

Are there any others?

These are the only kind manufactured in our own country, but Turkey, Persian and Axminster are also used.

How is the ingrain variety made?

There are two distinct webs, having two sets of woollen weft, and two of worsted warp.

How are these webs united?

The warp threads pass from one to the other so as to bring the required colors to the surface, two only being generally used in this kind.

How does the " three-ply " differ?

There are three webs, making the carpet thicker; more colors can also be used.

What can you say of Brussels and tapestry carpets?

At first it was thought impossible to weave them except by hand; however, the work can now be done by power looms.

What advantage has resulted?

Before this improvement, only 4 yards could be made in a day, now 20 yds. are produced in the same time of much better quality, so as to surpass those of any other country.

To whom are we indebted for the use of the power loom?

This is the work of Mr. Bigelow, of Lowell, Mass.,

who has brought the business to its present state of perfection.

Why are Brussels carpets so called?

They were named from the capital of Belgium, being first made there, and then introduced into England in the last century.

How is Brussels carpeting made?

There are usually five or more colors in the thread, woven upon a ground of heavy linen weft.

How do the colors run?

Usually the length of the web, and are so managed that all those required for the pattern are brought up together across the line of the carpet.

Before they are drawn down what is done?

A wooden instrument, called a "sword," is passed through to hold up the threads, this is replaced by a wound wire, which being removed, leaves an even row of loops, as can be easily seen on a piece of the carpet.

What causes it to be so thick?

As one color only appears in its place on the surface, all the rest remain beneath, making it very heavy.

How does the Wilton carpet differ from the Brussels?

The loops are cut before the wire is removed; there is a groove in the wire to receive the edge of the knife, that the cutting may be perfectly even. This is what gives the carpet its velvety appearance.

How are tapestry carpets made?

They are two-ply, the colors for the figures being printed on the yarn before weaving.

*When the yarn for the carpets leaves the spinning
jacks, how does it look?*

It is very coarse, tightly rolled on large spools, from
these it is wound into skeins and ready for the dye-
house.

What is done there?

Some of the skeins to be used for warp, are dyed
so as to have half-a-dozen different colors in each one,
this is done by a peculiar way of folding and tying the
yarn. The other bundles are dyed according to the
various colors required.

What is done with them then?

They are thoroughly dried in rooms directly over
the engine boilers, and wound upon spools and bobbins, by winding machines, worked by girls.

What then follows?

The thread is immediately wound upon immense
cylinders; each filling of the roller makes but one
thread in the warp of a single pattern, so that if there
are 208 threads in the width of a single piece of carpet, the roller must be filled as many times, and also
carefully printed.

How is the yarn printed?

Under the cylinder there is another roller, which
lays on each shade, in straight lines passing across, so
that when all are printed there are sometimes 100 or
more shades of colors.

What is done then?

The skeins are carefully packed in boxes containing rice-chaff; a little rail-road car, takes them to the

boiler, where they are subjected to the pressure of steam. The colors are then *fixed*, according to the process already described, and the yarn is ready for the weaver. After that the carpet is rolled very smooth by machines, marked, labelled and ready for sale.

CHAPTER III.

SHODDY.

Within a few years we have heard much of a kind of cloth called shoddy: what is it?

Although generally regarded as worthless, yet it is applied to many useful purposes, and when sold under its real name is worth the price paid for it.

Is it ever passed off in the market for any thing else?

Yes; as it can be made to resemble good cloth, Shoddy is frequently sold for a prime article.

Where was it first made?

As the Americans are said to cheat a little now and then in trade, we would suppose shoddy must have originated here, but such is not the case; we are indebted to the English for the invention, although we have six or more factories for making the article.

In what part of England did the business commence?

At the little village of Dewsbury, in Yorkshire, which has now become a flourishing town of some 30,000 inhabitants; the rapid increase within the past twenty years is owing to this business alone.

What can you say of the warehouses erected for the purpose?

They are immense stone buildings, and on entering the principal one, there are seen hundreds of bales of cast-off clothing, collected from various parts of Europe.

How are these obtained?

Agents are constantly travelling round, either buying or begging old clothes, from the rich and poor, the noblemen as well as the peasant; as far as possible all are of woollen.

What is done with these garments?

Dewsbury seems to be the head-quarters for the sale of them to the manufacturers in other parts of the kingdom, who constantly apply for the article.

When the agents bring in their collections to the warehouse what is done with them?

They are carefully assorted into, "shawls," "carpets," "black cloth," "stockings," "linseys," etc., etc., and then offered to the highest bidder.

What prices are often paid for them?

White flannel will often bring $100 a ton, old stockings from $35 to $50, black cloth from $100 to $150, and coarse mixed goods from $15 to $25 per ton.

When taken to the manufacturer what is done with the goods?

They are very carefully assorted, so that the woollen shall be separated from the cotton or other materials, when it is passed into the rag machine.

What is done with it there?

By means of a cylinder, armed with steel teeth half an inch apart, the rags are torn into wool, which can be spun and woven like the ordinary article.

What is "mungo"?

It is a better kind of cloth made from that which is of a superior quality, greater care is taken also to have the wool finer and more fleecy before spinning.

Is the wool there made into cloth?

No; it is usually packed away for sale at the market, where it is readily bought. The "mungo" often brings 8 pence English, per pound, and the shoddy from one to sixpence; a penny being equal to about two cents.

What has been done to remove the roughness of the "shoddy," as the wool itself is called in Yorkshire?

At first oil was used, but for some time milk has been substituted, answering the purpose very well.

What change in the price of milk?

It is sold for twice as much as before:

What kind of cloth is made out of the shoddy?

The white is used for light colored goods, the dark for carpets, coarse cloths, which are dyed any dark color to hide the various shades formed by the different fabrics of which it is made ; new wool is sometimes added to improve the quality.

How can shoddy be soon told from any other kind of cloth?

After wearing a short time, the wool will rub out, fall off, and the rest becomes useless.

Is there any advantage in making shoddy ?

It can be sold much cheaper than any other kind of cloth, besides that which would otherwise be useless, can be turned to some account. Much deception is however liable to be practiced in the business.

SECTION VIII.

CHAPTER I.

SILK.—EARLY HISTORY.

When and by whom was silk probably first used?

It is supposed that the Chinese were the first to engage in the manufacture of it, but when they began doing so is unknown.

At what time did it appear in other countries?

The silk, already woven, was brought from Persia to Greece 325 B. C., and later to Rome; even in the time of the emperor Tiberius, 300 years afterwards it was considered a criminal act of extravagance, especially for men, to wear silk.

When was the first silk garment worn in Rome?

In A. D. 229 by Heliogabalus. Silk was at first valued the same as gold, weight for weight.

When were the first silk-worms brought to Europe?

In the 6th century; some say the eggs were car ried from China to Constantinople by a monk in the hollow part of his cane, as the law strictly forbade any eggs or worms to be taken from China, under penalty of death.

What progress was made in the manufacture of the article?

At first very little; for it was not until the time of Francis I., about 1510, that it was introduced into Italy, Spain and the south of France. In 1688 some French refugees brought the business to perfection in England, at Spitalsfields, where a very flourishing trade is now carried on.

From what is silk obtained?

It is taken from the cocoons of the caterpillar, of the mulberry tree moth ; some varieties are also made from the cocoons of other insects.

Can you mention any of them ?

The thread produced by the *Saturina Cynthia,* are woven and spun into white cloth, which though of a loose texture, is yet so durable as to be scarcely worn out in the lifetime of a single person.

Has the spider's web ever been used ?

Attempts were made to weave it, but the quantity made by the spiders is so small, and the difficulty of rearing them so great, as they are very quarrelsome, that, like some persons, more time is spent in fighting and blood-shed than in useful labor, therefore the attempt has been abandoned.

Was any thing ever made of the spider's web?

Many years ago a pair of gloves and stockings were produced as a curiosity.

Does the silk-worm spin while it is in the caterpillar state ?

It does not usually commence until it is about 32 days old, and ready to become a chrysalis.

What is a chrysalis ?

It is the state into which insects pass from the form of worms before becoming winged, as moths, wasps, butterflies, etc.

What takes place during that time ?

The insect weaves a covering for its body, some times very smooth on the outer part, and sometimes rough or silky.

Before weaving the silk, does the caterpillar undergo any change ?

Yes; it sheds its skin four times. By increasing the heat it will do this in about half the usual time.

Explain the method of spinning the thread.

The silk gum used for the purpose, forms after the last moulting or change of skin. Before that, the caterpillar eats greedily, but now the appetite diminishes as the spinning commences, during which time it eats little or nothing.

Where is the spinning apparatus ?

It is placed near the mouth of the worm, which is joined to the bags of silk gum, that are closed below and end in very delicate tubes, one on each side of a bag, these all unite and form a single spinning tube, through which the gum is drawn : each thread of silk has two strands.

How does the work begin ?

The caterpillar first makes an outer covering of floss silk, to keep off the rain, a roll of paper or some thing is usually furnished where it can retire, as it will always hide itself, when in the wild state.

What then follows ?

It spins a finer web within the first, entirely covering the body to protect it from the cold and storms, and then still another within this, finer than the last, glued so firmly together that not even the air can enter.   This is the cocoon.

What does the worm then become ?

It passes into the chrysalis state, after that becomes a moth, when it bursts through its three coverings and comes out.

How does a cocoon look ?

It is about the size of a pigeon's egg, of a bright yellow color.

How long before the moth comes out of the cocoon ?

The time varies from 15 to 56 days, according to the temperature.   In the Southern States about 15 days, in Connecticut, 18 to 20.   In France, three weeks, and in England, 5 or 6.   The cocoon can be made in a few hours, although sometimes 2 or 3 days are necessary.

What mistakes will the caterpillar sometimes make?

Two or three will shut themselves up in the same cocoon, but this does not seem to make any difference, the usual work and changes go on the same as ever.

How is the silk unwound when covered with glue?

Sometimes the cocoons are thrown into boiling water, but as this, of course, kills the chrysalis, they can be steamed without any injury to the insect; the glue is then softened so that the silk can be easily unwound, and the moth comes forth alive to lay its eggs, etc.

What is necessary for success in raising silk-worms?

To secure warmth, dryness, pure air, and plenty of proper food; the leaves of the mulberry tree form its chief nourishment.

Do any other insects use the same food?

It is said that none but the silk-worm feed upon it, therefore the insect and tree must have been created for each other.

What peculiar kind of worm in India?

There is one much valued by the Hindoos, as it produces a coarse, dark-colored silk highly esteemed by them.

Are these reared in the usual way?

No; they are very wild, so that the natives are obliged to leave the caterpillars on their trees and guard them from the birds by day, and from the bats at night.

CHAPTER II.

GENERAL PROGRESS.

We have already referred to the use of silk in Europe, when was the first successful silk factory established there ?

In 1564, at Nimes, in France ; since then the business has rapidly increased in the southern part of the country, the climate seeming better adapted to raising the worms.

What did James I. of England urge his subjects to do ?

He tried to induce them to follow the example of their French neighbors.

Did they comply with the King's wishes ?

Many attempts were made to rear the silk-worm, but the climate was not adapted to it, although in Russia and Germany, where it is much colder, the business was quite successful.

When was the first silk-mill erected in England ?

In 1718, by John Lombe, who, disguised as a common workman, obtained access to the mills at Pied-

mont in Italy ; having acquired the necessary knowledge, and bribed some of the workmen to join him,
they returned secretly to England.

What followed ?

A large mill was at once erected at Derby, five
stories high, $\frac{1}{8}$ of a mile long, contained 26,586 spinning wheels, that would produce 73,726 yds. of silk
thread at every revolution of the water-wheel, which
turned once in three minutes.

Did this attempt prove a success ?

Yes ; it was very profitable, although the quality of
the silk did not equal that made upon the continent.
But in 1824, many improvements in machines, etc.,
were introduced, that made a much better fabric than
before, so that more than $600,000, worth of goods
were exported from England to France.

How was the silk-worm brought to America ?

When James I. found it could not be reared in
England, he thought it might succeed in his colonies,
and therefore sent some eggs to Virginia as an experiment.

What success followed?

Although great rewards were offered if the object
could be accomplished, yet other products proved so
much more profitable, the silk culture declined and
was at length abandoned.

*What can you mention as made of the silk produced
in Virginia ?*

The coronation robe of Charles II. was made of it
in 1660.

Were there any attempts in other parts of the country?

Yes; in the 18th century efforts were made in nearly all the colonies. The culture was introduced into Louisiana in 1718, special artists were sent from different parts of Europe to Georgia, to instruct the Americans in rearing the worms and winding the silk. Mulberry trees and eggs were also furnished, and grants of land offered to those who would engage in the work.

What was then adopted?

A State seal was struck, representing silk worms at work, and bearing the generous motto: " *Non sibi, sed alius* " " Not for ourselves, but others."

What interrupted the work in Georgia?

The agent from Piedmont, Mr. Amatis, having produced some silk equal to the Italian and French, became dissatisfied, fearing probably that America might rival his own country, and so destroyed all the machinery, trees and eggs, then fled to Carolina.

What followed?

His place was soon filled by another Italian who took charge of a " filature " there, that is a place where the silk is unwound from the cocoons.

When was the first raw silk exported?

In 1743, when Gen. Oglethorpe took 8 lbs. to England; the next year more was sent, made into a dress for Queen Caroline to be worn at a levée, on the King's birthday.

What success followed?

At Ebenezer, on the Savannah, a large establishment was erected, and from 1760 to 1768, 100,000 lbs. of cocoons were delivered at the filature.   But owing to the bounty being withdrawn by the English gov ernment, the business declined and entirely ceased at the time of the Revolutionary War.   The last lot of silk, 200 lbs., was sold in Georgia in 1790.

Why was not the business renewed there at the close of the war?

The cultivation of cotton is found so much more profitable, there is but little chance for the silk culture. The soil and climate are however so well adapted to it, that in time the business may be revived.

In what other state was silk cultivated successfully?

In S. Carolina both as a business and an amusement.

What can you say of Mrs. Pinckney?

She was the mother of some of the Revolutionary generals.   With her own hands she had spun and woven a quantity of excellent silk.

What was done with it?

The lady herself took it to England where three complete dresses were made of the silk.   One was presented to the Princess of Wales, and another to Lord Chesterfield.

Did the business always flourish in S. Carolina?

No ; it was brought to a close by the war, as in Georgia.

Did the silk trade ever revive?

Yes; although interrupted for a time by the war, it was again renewed, the Northern States even engag-ing in the business.

When were silk fabrics produced there ?

The first silk coat and stockings made in New England were worn in 1747 by Gov. Law, and in 1750 his daughter appeared in a dress of the same material.

Was the business found profitable ?

It must have been, for in 1789, at Mansfield, Conn., 200 lbs. of raw silk were manufactured, which was worth $5.00 per. lb. This was made into ribbons, handkerchiefs, stockings, sewing silk, etc., the latter selling for $1.00 per. oz.

Is the silk trade still carried on at the North ?

Yes; in many of the New England States, the mulberry tree seems to flourish. The finest nursery in the country some years since, being that of Dr. Stebbins at Northampton, Mass., and much success has attended the manufacture, but not sufficient as yet to make it as desirable as many other employments.

What was done at Auburn, N. Y ?

In 1841, the convicts at the State Prison there, produced sewing-silk, worth $12,762.

How does the article made here compare with that in other countries ?

It is equal to the Chinese, and superior to much of the European.

What can you say of the present condition of the business in this country ?

The manufactory of Cheney Bros., commenced at Manchester, N. H., and soon after at Hartford, Conn., employed, in 1870, 1000 hands, and produced 120,000 lbs. of silk thread, 100,000 pieces of belt ribbons, and 600,000 yds. of wide dress silks, besides making the best sewing silk in the country.

Can you mention any other places where the trade also flourishes ?

At Paterson, N. J., there are 15 factories. In the State of N. J. nearly $2,000,000 worth of goods are produced annually ; and in the U. S. to the amount of $18,000,000.

Do we import as much as formerly ?

No ; far less, and before long, we may be able to obtain all we need from the home market.

What reason for this supposition ?

It had been ascertained that the finest raw silk in the world can be obtained from California. In 1870 12,000,000 cocoons were produced there.

What is now being done to increase the business ?

Groves of mulberry trees have been planted in many places, and every effort made to improve the quality as well as quantity of the silk.

Is the climate adapted to the worm ?

It is found equal to that of any other State, in fact the moth is healthier there than elsewhere; three generations can be raised in a single season.

CHAPTER III.

METHOD OF MAKING SILK.

When the cocoons are perfectly formed, what is done with them?

They are collected together and carefully assorted. Some of the best are kept for breeding, others used for the waste, as will be soon explained, and the rest are divided according to their qualities, so that each kind can be worked by itself.

What follows?

Before the moth has life enough to eat its way out of the cocoon, it must be destroyed, which is done by exposing it to the heat of the sun, or of an oven ; sometimes hot water and steam are also used.

What is necessary in doing this?

Great care is taken not to have the heat too great, as the quality of the silk might be injured, or even made worthless.

How is it known when the insects are dead?

By opening a few of the cocoons to see if the chrysalis shows any signs of life when pricked with a pin.

What is the next step ?

If the insect is dead, the covering is opened at one end, the cocoon slipped out, when the process of unwinding begins.

Is this usually done at the same place ?

No ; the cocoons are taken to the "filatures," and sold, there the work goes on. Great care is required to do it well, as the thread may become easily entangled or broken.

Explain the process ?

The cocoons are thrown into troughs having 4 divisions, about 5 insects in each. These are filled with warm water to dissolve the gummy substance on the silk.

What is the next step ?

They are stirred with a little broom, which catches a thread from each, all of them being then united, are drawn through a small eyelet to remove any of the gum that may remain ; still more is taken off by making the threads cross and rub against each other as they pass through several more eyelets on to the reel.

Are the silk fibers still separate ?

No ; they have become united into one thread, which is wound on the reel in regular spirals, going from one end to the other, so that one thread does not overlay the other before the row is finished.

Why is it done in this way ?

Because if any gum still remained on the fiber it will have a chance to dry, that the next row of threads may not stick to it.

How is the same size of thread obtained ?

New cocoons are added before the first are quite unwound, as the inner part of the fiber is much finer than the other.

Is the thread wound round and round upon the cocoon in spinning ?

No; it is passed back and forth in one place after another, so that many yards can sometimes be taken off without turning over the ball.

What is the size of each fiber as it comes out of the spinning bag ?

About $\frac{1}{2000}$ of an inch.

What is the color of the raw silk ?

It is usually a bright golden color, and consists of many filaments slightly twisted together ; this is called a single thread. By pulling apart a piece of floss, the size and delicacy of the fiber can be easily seen.

How much silk is produced by a single cocoon ?

One of a good size yields about 300 yds. of filament, and some even 600 yds. Usually 11 or 12 lbs. of cocoons are allowed for one of raw silk.

What is done with the silk when taken from the reels ?

In China it is made up into bundles, called " books," but in other countries the hanks are simply twisted so as to remain snugly together, and are then ready for " throwing."

Explain the meaning of that term ?

" Throwing " signifies the different kinds of twist

formed from the reeled silk, according to the use made of it.

Give some examples?

If the thread is for bandanna handkerchiefs, the hanks are only wound and cleaned. If for gauze and similar fabrics it is also bleached. That intended for ribbons and common silks is " thrown," or twisted once ; when doubled before twisting it is called " tram," and is used for the wool of velvets and flower-ed silks. The warp is made from the "organzine " thread as it is called, which has been twisted in each strand before doubling, as well as afterwards.

What can you say of " organzine " silk ?

It is the strongest and most durable that is made.

What is done with the hanks before winding ?

They are washed in soap and water ; when the bob-bins are filled from the reels the silk passes through the " cleaner."

How does this work ?

The full bobbins are set on spindles which, being put in motion, each thread passes over a glass or iron rod, that guides it between two upright blades, on to another set of bobbins which are soon filled.

How does the " cleaner." act upon the thread ?

It rubs off any knots or roughness on the silk : if some still remain, the bobbin will not move until the thread is made perfectly smooth by the hand of the operator.

After cleaning what next takes place ?

The silk is spun and twisted by machines similar to

those used for spinning cotton. The thread is colored by dyeing as soon as the gum has been removed; for this purpose it is first boiled three or four hours in soap and water.

What is done with the " waste " silk?

That is put aside until there is enough to use, as it gradually accumulates during the making of the other silk. It is then hackled or combed out, first by hand, afterward by machinery, as described for cotton, the impurities are thus removed; the fibers are cut into pieces about $1\frac{1}{4}$ inches long, these are combed still more.

How does the silk look now?

It resembles a soft downy fleece, which is boiled for an hour and a half in soap and water, then in pure water, when it is squeezed by a powerful press and dried by the fire or steam pipes. It is once more scutched or combed, then is ready for carding, drawing, etc., as already described.

What is made of it?

The waste silk is used for shawls, bandanna handkerchiefs, and similar articles.

How does a thread of silk compare with one of hemp or flax?

Although so fine and delicate, it is much stronger and more durable. To the little silk-worm, therefore, we are indebted for some of our most useful and beautiful fabrics.

CHAPTER I.

INDIA RUBBER.

Is the manufacture of India Rubber an old or new invention?

The uses to which it may be applied were not known to Europeans 150 years ago, so that it is a comparatively modern invention, although the natives of the countries where it is found have used it for ages in a rude fashion.

To whom are we indebted for this discovery ?

The French astronomers sent to Peru in 1735, were the first to call attention to this useful article. In 1751, the tree was discovered by Frisman, in Cayenne.

Where is it found most abundantly ?

In the Province of Para, in Brazil, immense quantities are obtained.

What is India Rubber?

Caoutchouc,* or India Rubber, is the thickened

* Pronounced Koo-chook.

FICUS ELASTICA,
From which India Rubber is obtained.

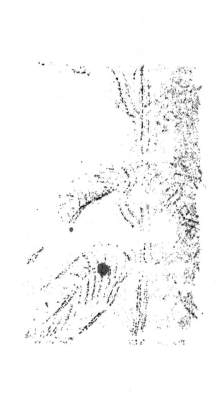

milky juice of various trees and plants found in Brazil, Guiana, Peru, East Indies, etc. A similar substance is obtained from the Poppy-lettuce.

Are the trees found in S. America like those in the East Indies ?

No ; they differ somewhat. One species, the *ficus elastica,* found in Asia, grows to a great size, measuring sometimes 74 feet in circumference and 100 feet in height.

What may be seen at Assam ?

At Assam, beyond the Ganges, immense forests of these trees are found, but the quality of the India Rubber is inferior to that of S. America. In the latter country the best species is the " Siphonica Elastica," which grows to a height of 60 or 70 feet, and is covered with a scaly bark.

What does it bear?

It produces a fruit, which encloses a kind of white almond, much esteemed by the natives.

How is the sap obtained from the tree ?

By tapping it slightly, the juice flows freely, which is thick, white and oily, like that of the milk-weed.

How is it hardened ?

By exposure to the air, it soon becomes solid.

How is the sap collected?

The natives cut the trees lengthwise, also making incisions on each side of the long one that lead to it, so that the juice flows from all parts of the tree at the same time, into a bandanna leaf at the bottom ; from this it passes into the vessels placed to receive it.

What is then done with it ?

The natives were accustomed to make moulds in clay, of shoes, cups, jars and other articles. While the sap was still fluid, it was poured over these moulds, then dried by fire or in the sun—when it would retain the desired form.

How were the moulds taken out?

By soaking in water, they became loosened and could be easily removed.

In what form did India Rubber first appear in the U. S. ?

Clumsy overshoes were made of it, and imported from Para. Little square pieces were also sold for erasing lead pencil marks, at 50c. for $\frac{1}{2}$ cubic inch.

How were candles made of it ?

The wick being first dipped in tallow and allowed to harden, the sap was applied as in the case of moulds. The natives also make it into tubes for holding sticks that can be used as torches.

When dried by the sun what is the color ?

It is white within and yellowish-brown without. If the heat of fire is used, the smoke makes it black, as we usually see it.

Does the India Rubber dry quickly?

No ; several days' exposure to the sun will be required. During this time it is so soft that various fanciful figures can be marked upon it with a stick.

Why is the name " syringe " sometimes given to the tree ?

This was applied by the Portuguese, both to the

gum and the tree, from a peculiar custom of the natives, who presented their guests after meals with one
of the Indian rubber bottles, having a hollow stem attached to it, for squirting the water into their mouths.

What was the difficulty at first in using the gum ?

The ingenious Americans having discovered how
useful it might be made, could not find anything that
would dissolve it, as the Caoutchouc differed from all
gums then known ; being like resin it would not dissolve in alcohol.

After various experiments what was the result?

It was at length found to be soluble in volatile
oils ?

What are volatile oils ?

Those that will evaporate when exposed to the air,
as oil of cloves, lavender, etc., etc.   Such as will not
thus waste away are called "*fixed ;* " whale, coal and
castor oils are examples of the latter.

*By mixing the gum with a volatile oil what was
formed ?*

A kind of varnish, very useful in making cloth, etc.,
water-proof.

How was it applied ?

A thin coat, placed between two pieces of cloth,
made them adhere closely together, so as to be both
air tight and water proof.

What articles were made in this way ? ·

Bottles, boots, pillows, cushions, mattresses, etc.
By dissolving the gum in linseed oil, an excellent varnish for leather was obtained.

Can you mention anything else that would act as a solvent?

A preparation of the rubber itself, called Caout-choucin.*

How is it made?

When the gum is exposed to a heat of 600°, it will pass off into vapor : if this is condensed, it will become the solvent required.

What other difficulty attended the use of Caoutchouc?

All the experiments made with it at first were obliged to be carried on in its native country, because the pure juice quickly spoiled when not used at once.

How was this difficulty remedied?

Mr. Lee Norris, of New York, devised a plan by which it could be transported any distance without injury.

Explain it.

The liquor was first filtered or strained, then mixed with about one-eighth of its own weight of ammonia, which preserves it from the effect of the air. When necessary to use the mixture, it is poured out on some smooth surface, already shaped as required, and exposed to 70° or 100° of heat ; the ammonia will evaporate, leaving the gum smooth and hard on the mould

To what uses thus far had India Rubber been applied?

Mostly for purposes where elasticity, or water-proof qualities were required.

Pron. Koo-chookin.

Mention some articles made from it ?

Water-proof cloth, surgical instruments, elastic bands, etc. Book binders also used it for securing the leaves of books, so as to open easily. When in thin sheets, impressions of engravings have been taken. It is also used for covering the mouths of bottles to exclude water and air. A kind of marine glue has been made of it.

How is this done ?

The rubber is dissolved in coal-tar naptha, and well mixed. In ten or twelve days it becomes as thick as cream : shellac is then added, when the whole is heated in an iron vessel having a pipe at the bottom. While melting, it is stirred ; the liquid then flows out through the pipe, and is obtained in the form of thin sheets.

How is the glue used?

It is heated and then applied with a brush to the parts that are to be joined together; heated rollers pass over the surface, so that the work may be well done.

What can you say of this glue?

It holds so firmly, that when masts of vessels have been joined by it, they will break in some other part before a fracture takes place where it has been used. Even some say that it is stronger than iron bolts, and may be substituted for them.

What other uses can you mention ?

Stables, lobbies, and halls in this country, as well as in England, have been paved with rubber. The car-

riage-way of Windsor Castle is so paved. It is also
used for making bath-tubs, dishes for photograph and
chemical purposes, telegraph-wire covers, boots, shoes,
life-preservers, toys, bags, tents, beds, buckets, etc.,
etc. New applications of it are constantly being
made.

*What difficulty may still be mentioned, that had to be
overcome before it could become of even far greater ser-
vice than ever before ?*

Thus far, it had merely been used as the raw material,
in its native condition ; it was necessary to change the
nature of the substance itself, as to make something
new of it.

Had any attempts been made to accomplish this ?

Yes ; repeated experiments were tried by the wisest
men, but their skill seemed baffled.

*Who at length succeeded in accomplishing the
work ?*

This honor is due to Mr. Charles Goodyear, of New
York.

Was the discovery made by accident ?

No ; it was the result of 20 YEARS' constant toil and
perseverance ! An example worthy of imitation by
scholars, who are apt to be discouraged, after trying
even one short hour, to master a difficult problem,
hard lesson, or some other similar trouble.

What was the result of this patient labor ?

Mr. Goodyear discovered that if sulphur and white
lead were mixed with the caoutchouc, and exposed to
regular heat for 8 or 12 hours, it becomes *vulcanized.*

What is the meaning of vulcanized ?

It is a term applied to the change that takes place in caoutchouc when united with sulphur, producing an entirely new substance, and unlike any other, so that, whatever affected the rubber before, as heat and cold, has no power over it now.

What other difference between the two ?

The new article cannot be dissolved by the same liquids as the natural gum. It becomes much more elastic than before, and may now be called an " elastic metal."

What is the nature of the mixture when put in the heaters ?

It is a tough, sticky, unelastic dough. On coming out it is very elastic, can be easily handled, and adapted to nearly all the purposes of life.

CHAPTER II.

PROCESS OF MANUFACTURE.

When the raw material is imported, in what condition is it found?

It is usually in thick lumps, mixed with leaves, dirt and sticks, so that when cleaned it loses about one-fifth of its weight.

What is first done with it?

A large vat being filled with hot water, the rubber is thrown in, and remains until the outer part is soft enough to take off the basket work that covers it.

What follows?

By means of powerful machinery, a circular knife cuts the lumps into slabs about an inch thick; these are then placed in the "cracker."

What is that?

The name is given to a machine having two large cylinders, with grooves running lengthwise. The sheets of rubber being placed between them are torn and twisted to pieces, so that much of the dirt and sticks work out.

What now takes place ?

It is taken to the washing machine, where many small knives, revolving under the water, cut the rubber into small pieces, which at the same time are kneaded and thoroughly cleansed, being then ready for the grinding machine.

How does this work ?

The grinding machine consists of large hollow cylinders made of cast iron. As these turn in opposite directions, the rubber is kneaded and pressed into thick sheets or mats.

Can this be used at once?

No; it must first be cured, or thoroughly dried in the air, which requires several months. As the manufacturers keep a large supply of the material on hand, the other parts of the work still go on.

When the sheets are cured, what is done with them ?

They are put in the mixing machines, where they are united with metals and other substances, by means of very large and strong cylinders, that knead the rubber like dough.

How are they heated ?

Steam is let in at each end of the rollers, which are hollow.

What noise is heard during this operation ?

Constant explosions, like pistol-shots, caused by the air in the folds of the rubber, forced out by the cylinders. It is on the same principle as that which makes a little piece of rubber, that has been chewed,

explode, when struck on the hand ; a favorite amuse
ment with children.

What are the substances mixed with the rubber ?

Sulphur, with oxides of iron, zinc, lead, and other
metals.

Is this an easy part of the operation ?

No, very difficult ; as greater care and skill are required than in any other portion of the work.

Why is this so ?

Because each quality of rubber requires different
compounds, as well as different treatment in the various steps of the manufacture.

*When the substance is thus prepared, what can be
done with it ?*

It may now be moulded into any shape that is desired, the method depending of course upon the various uses to be made of it : whether designed for a
comb, a carpet, steam valve, door-spring, or any of the
many articles that are made of it.

*What can you say of the English method of cleansing
the rubber ?*

It is similar to the American. The power of their
cylinder machine seems even greater than ours.

How does this appear?

The friction of the rollers against the caoutchouc
is so great that the cold water put in to wash it will
soon boil ; for we know the greater the friction between substances, the more heat is set free.

How is the rubber hardened, as that used for combs, canes, buttons, knife-handles, etc. ?

A preparation of bone, shell, ivory or magnesia is mixed with the caoutchouc.

How is rubber formed into threads ?

When it is kneaded into sheets, long fine strips are cut off by knives kept wet and worked with machines ; these can be joined together by cutting each of the two ends smoothly and obliquely ; then pressing them with the fingers they will unite very quickly and firmly.

What change takes place in the thread when it is reeled off?

By passing through the moistened fingers of a boy, it is stretched out nearly eight times longer than before, ceases to be elastic, and remains upon the reels about eight days.

What is then done with it ?

The threads being wound upon bobbins, are ready for weaving, braiding, etc.

Are all equally fine ?

No ; there are different qualities, according to the use to be made of them.

How can India Rubber cloth, cord, etc., be elastic, if the thread has lost its elasticity by stretching as just described ?

The rubber thread, when stretched, is woven with silk, cotton or whatever other material may be required, after which a hot iron being passed over the fabric the elasticity is restored at once. The rubber returns to its former length, drawing up with it the materials woven in, thus giving the shirred appearance always seen.

Are the different articles made from rubber all manufactured at the same place?

No; as some require larger and more powerful machines, as well as different methods and materials, there are various factories for the separate branches of the business.

Give an example of one.

The manufacture of "belting" is a very important item in the Rubber Mills, as it can be made stronger than any leather produced.

For what is it used?

Belting forms the bands we see passing around large and small wheels of all kinds of machinery. If it was not made very strong, great damage might be done by the breaking of these bands. It will adhere to the pulley so closely that there is never any danger of slipping off, as is the case with leather.

Of what is the belting made?

"Cotton duck," a strong kind of cotton cloth, is used for the foundation, being woven so as to have twice the usual strength in its length. By means of powerful machines, the rubber is forced into the meshes of the duck.

What is now done with it?

The cloth thus prepared, is passed through the calender machine, where a coating of rubber is rolled upon it, in a perfectly smooth sheet, so pressed and heated in, that it becomes a part of the cloth itself.

What follows ?

It is taken to the belt-room, spread upon tables 100 feet long, and cut into strips of various widths, according to the kind of belting required.

If belts of great strength are made what is done ?

Several of the strips are pressed together by immense rolling machines, making them strong as metal and more serviceable, as they are not affected by heat, cold, or moisture.

Are they now ready to use ?

No ; they must pass into the "heaters," which are long steam boilers. The door being opened, a railway carriage is drawn out, the goods are placed on this and rolled back into the boiler, which is now closed and the steam admitted.

How long do they remain there ?

From 8 to 12 hours, when they become "vulcanized;" or changed from rubber and cloth into a material differing from either

What other very useful article can you mention made of similar materials ?

The "Croton hose" for fire engines and other water purposes.

How is it made ?

A long iron tube, from ⅛ to 12 inches in diameter, is covered with a sheet of rubber very carefully prepared. Over this are layers of cloth similar to belting-duck. When there are folds enough to give it the required strength, an outer covering of pure rubber is added.

What follows ?

The pipes with the hose on them are placed in immense heaters, where the steam is let on as above described for belting.   When they have become vulcanized, the pipes are removed from the hose, which is then tested.   If of the proper strength, it will stand a pressure that would burst the strongest leather pipe.

Can you mention any other use to which this peculiar kind of rubber cloth is applied?

The immense valves of ocean steamers, sometimes five feet in diameter, are made of it.

What is the great wonder connected with India Rubber?

That one single substance can be applied to so many uses, for which nothing else will answer the same purpose, and that finding it so very useful, we could have done without it so long.

Are there any other uses to be made of it?

Doubtless ; very many of which we have never dreamed, as new ways of applying it are discovered every day.   No other discovery or invention was ever made that advanced so rapidly and became so generally useful as that of caoutchouc.

CHAPTER III.

GUTTA PERCHA.

What substance has been discovered closely resembling Caoutchou?

Gutta Percha. It is so called from Gutta, meaning a gum, and Percha, the name of a tree. The Malays, however, call it "*Gutta tuban.*"

Where is the tree found?

It grows in large forests at the foot of the hills in the peninsula of Malay, and forms the principal part of the jungle in the lowlands. It is also found in Borneo and other islands of the Indian archipelago.

Describe the tree.

It is quite large, from 3 to 6 ft. in diameter, grows to the height of 60 or 70 ft. The gum collects in cavities running the length of the tree. This flows out when the tree is tapped like caoutchouc. The natives, however, always gathered it by first cutting down the tree, as they knew nothing of tapping.

How many trees were thus sacrificed?

In about a year and a-half 69,180 trees were cut down to obtain a little over 9,000 lbs. of the Gutta.

Has this article been known for a long time ?

The Malayans knew of its valuable properties long
before the Europeans found out that it would become
soft when put in hot water, and if then moulded would
retain whatever shape was given it.

For what purposes did they make it ?

It was formed into shoes, basins, vases, whips,
handles for axes, etc.

*When was the attention of Europeans first called to
it ?*

In 1842, Dr. Wm. Montgomerie, a surgeon at
Singapore, also another physician the next year,
brought specimens of Gutta Percha to England.

Did it attract much attention ?

Not at first ; but as Dr. Voss showed that it could
be used for almost the same purposes as caoutchouc,
as well as others, and might be obtained in great
quantities at little cost, people became interested in
it.

How rapidly did the business progress ?

The first shipment of 2 cwt. was made from Singapore in 1844, and in little more than four years nearly
3,000,000 lbs. were exported, of which almost half
came to the United States.

How does Gutta Percha differ from Caoutchouc?

It does not become elastic as rubber, although when
heated it may be made quite flexible, and if the heat
is increased, can be drawn into threads or tubes and
rolled into thin plates, which retain their form when
cold.

Is the gum easily dissolved?

No ; there are few liquids that have any effect upon it. Oil of turpentine will dissolve it partially when cold. Ether may also be used for the same purpose if there is no alchohol in either of them.

What is the most important use made of it ?

As the Gutta Percha, when dry, is a bad conductor of electricity, it is found very suitable for coating the submarine telegraph wires, that is, those that pass under water.

Of what is it composed?

Carbon, hydrogen and oxygen form the substance, these elements being the same as in Caoutchouc, except that oxygen is wanting in the latter.

Can Gutta Percha be used for coating leather?

It is not found to answer the purpose as well as Caoutchouc, because the oils in the leather will decompose it ; but rubber not being affected by oils at all, is an admirable dressing.

What can you say of the process for preparing Gutta Percha?

It is similar to that already described for Caoutchouc, and can also be vulcanized, the process being different for the various articles to be made of it. It is found that by combining the Rubber and Gutta Percha, a still better material is obtained than either would furnish alone.

Can you mention some articles made of the latter?

They are almost innumerable ; as household utensils, ornaments in architecture, chemical apparatus, surgical instruments, parts of machinery, knapsacks, water-proof clothing, dolls, combs, clock cases, lining for sinks and cisterns, etc.

Can you mention any other very important use to which it is applied?

Life-boats are made of Gutta Percha, and have been found much stronger and more durable than any other kind.

Can you give an instance?

A boat of this material having a wooden frame was furnished by Lady Franklin to one of the Arctic expeditions, and although exposed to the roughest work of the voyage, came back to England in excellent condition.

Will you mention another?

In 1858 one was exhibited in New York having the ribs and keel all of the same piece as the rest of the boat.

How do surgeons find it very useful?

In making cases for diseased, fractured or deformed limbs.

How are they used?

The bands of Gutta Percha, 2 or 3 inches broad, are softened in hot water, then placed on the limb, when they become very firm and yet quite flexible.

Can you mention still another use made of it?

When Gutta Percha is dissolved and placed on a cut, it will firmly unite the edges, and if applied to flesh where the skin is removed, an artificial cuticle will be formed. Dentists also use it for temporary filling of teeth, as well as making plates of it for artificial ones.

What can you say of this discovery?

It is like Caoutchouc, one of the most important ever made, and in the few years it has been used, may be regarded as one of the most valuable articles of trade, and in connection with telegraphing, is almost indispensable, as nothing yet has been found for coating wires, to be used under the sea, so strong, durable, and able to resist the action of water as this.

SECTION X.

CHAPTER I.

CLOCKS AND WATCHES.

Were Clocks and Watches known to the ancients?

No; they may be classed among modern inventions.

How was time measured before Clocks were used?

The ancients marked its progress by the movement of the heavenly bodies, and measured it by the sun's shadow passing over a sun-dial.

How is a sun-dial made?

A circular piece of metal is divided into twelve equal parts like the face of a clock, and marked with the hours. This is laid upon a raised support, upon which is placed a piece of metal in the form of a triangle. When the sun shines, the shadow of the metal will fall exactly on the figure, marking the hour, and as the sun seems to move, the shadow of course does the same.

If it was cloudy what could the ancients substitute for the sun-dial?

A clepsydra, or water-clock, was then used. The

fluid flowed through a small hole in the bottom of a vessel into one beneath it.

How could this tell the time?

If the vessel was filled at noon, or any hour already known, as the water flowed out, the little marks on the inside would tell how much time had elapsed, by knowing how long it was in passing from one to the other.

In what other way was time measured?

By sand-glasses, the principle being the same in both. In the latter, sand was used instead of water.

Can you mention any other kind of Water-Clocks?

One was invented in the 17th century. It consists of a cylinder having small cells. This is hung by a thread fastened to the centre in a small frame on which the hours are marked.

How does it work?

The water flowing from one cell to another causes the center of gravity to change, and the cylinder of course moves accordingly, thus showing, by its position and certain marks, the required hour.

How did Alfred the Great measure time?

By means of candles which required a certain length of time to consume, and in order that the air might not affect their burning regularly, he had each candle covered with ox-horns, these being the first lanterns ever used.

When were clocks invented?

This is not certainly known. They appear to have been first used in Europe in the monasteries, about the 11th century ; the Saracens were probably the inventors.

What can you say of the Sultan of Egypt?

In 1232 he sent to the Emperor, Frederick II., a clock, or *horologium*, as it was called, having weights and wheels, not only showing the hour but also the movements of the heavenly bodies very exactly. In 1288, a clock was placed in Westminster Hall, probably the first one used in England.

What progress was made with this invention?

It must have been very slow ; for late in the 14th century, Charles V. of France engaged a German to put up a large striking clock in his palace. It had only one hand and would go but a single day.

Were Clocks at first large or small?

They were very large and could be used only in churches and monasteries. The wheels were at first three feet in diameter.

On what principle are Clocks and Watches made?

The principle which moves the works, is a contrivance, called an escapement, that regulates the action of the pendulum in clocks, or of the balance in watches, so that the former shall fall, and the latter unwind with exact regularity.

Why is it called an escapement?

Because it allows each tooth of the wheel that it holds, to escape at every vibration, which causes the ticking.

When was it first used?

It is not certainly known, although some say we

are indebted to Gerbert, a Frenchman, who lived about
A.D. 1000.

Who invented the pendulum ?

This honor is due to Galileo, and Richard Harris,
being constructed in 1641, although Huygens, a German, also claims to be the inventor. It is certain, at
least, that he did much towards making the use of it
more fully understood and generally applied.

*How does a pendulum regulate the movements of a
Clock ?*

The vibration or swinging of the pendulum causes
the motion of the wheel-work in the clock. If the
former vibrates rapidly or slowly, the latter will do the
same, making the clock go faster or slower as may be
desired.

*How can the movement of the pendulum be increased
or diminished ?*

By changing the length of the metal rod. If it is
to go faster, the pendulum must be shortened, if slower
it is lengthened.

*If it is once fixed the right length, will not the Clock
always keep exact time ?*

No ; for as heat expands and cold contracts metals,
as well as other things, the clock is apt to gain time
in winter, and lose it in summer, for the pendulum is
longer in summer than in winter, so that it must be
regulated accordingly.

*Can not some other kind of a pendulum be made that
will not be affected by the heat and cold?*

Various attempts have been made to do this. One

very ingenious contrivance of George Graham, in 1715 deserves to be mentioned.

Will you explain it?

He used a little tube of mercury instead of the pendulum ball. Now mercury when heated will rise in the tube, and sink when cold, so that it was found almost exactly to balance the lengthening of the rod in summer and the contraction in winter.

Can you mention still another contrivance?

In 1726, John Harrison made what was called the "Gridiron Pendulum." It was composed of 5 rods of steel and 4 of brass alternating with each other.

How did it work?

As brass dilates by heat and contracts by cold twice as much as steel, it was found that as the one set of rods by expanding, pushed the pendulum ball away from the point on which it was suspended, the other set by contraction drew it back. Each so counteracting the effect produced by the other, that perfect regularity in time was attained.

What other use did Harrison make of this principle?

He so applied it to the springs and wheels of watches, that the result was the same.

Did he obtain any reward for his invention?

The English Parliament gave him £20,000, this being the prize offered by the government for any one who could produce a perfect time-keeper.

Is there any fixed length for a pendulum?

It must be about 39 inches to beat seconds. In

small clocks the pendulum swings twice and some-times more in a second.

How can you best understand the movement of the escapement and pendulum ?

By examining a watch or clock while the works are still in motion. The whole mechanism will then appear very plain.

What nation has made the greatest progress in the art of Clock and Watch making ?

The Swiss watches have been usually regarded as the best ; many ingenious contrivances were introduced into them not found in those of other nations.

To what have the English directed their attention ?

They have devoted much time and care to the perfection of each part of the clock or watch, producing very elegant and costly specimens. The Americans, on the other hand, have sought to make theirs as cheap as possible, at the same time furnishing excellent and accurate time-pieces.

What great difference in the mode of manufacture ?

The English clocks are made by hand, those of America and France by machinery.

What can you say of the first Clocks that were made?

They were very large, and so expensive that only wealthy persons had them. Some were six or eight feet high, often without any case, except for the upper part. The weights nearly reached to the floor, and afforded children much amusement as they swung them back and forth, interfering sadly with the regularity of time.

13

CHAPTER II.

AMERICAN CLOCKS.

Where were Clocks first made in the U. S. ?

At the time of forming our government, Eli Terry of Windsor, Conn., made small clocks of wood to hang against the wall. In 1793 he established himself in the business, and in 1800 obtained the help of two young men.

How did they make these Clocks?

All the work was done by hand. The wheels were marked out with square and compass, then cut with a fine saw and jack-knife, the teeth being formed in the same way.

Where was their salesroom ?

They had none. But twice a year Mr. Terry would pack up the clocks he had made, and go into the "*new country*," to sell them at $25 each.

Where was the new country ?

This was the name given to the region west of the Hudson River. The clocks were then called "Wooden Movements."

What success attended these rude attempts?

His work was in such demand that in 1807 several of the citizens in Waterbury, Conn., formed a company to furnish Terry with materials for making the "*movements.*"

What then followed?

Having purchased an old mill, Mr. Terry fitted it with some machinery, and commenced making 500 clocks at once, which was more than any clock-maker in the world had ever attempted

What change took place in the price?

Formerly $25 had been paid for one. The price was now reduced to $20, $15, and finally, about 1811 or 1812, to $10 each.

Did Mr. Terry continue the business?

Although he sold his factory to Messrs. Thomas & Hadley, yet he afterwards resumed it.

What can you say of Mr. Thomas?

In 1813 he removed his business to Plymouth, the part of the town he occupied being called Thomas-town. He, with his sons and partners, have remained there up to the present time, and now carry on the largest clock manufactory in the world.

Where are their clocks used?

In every part of our own country, as well as in many others. We can hardly open the door of any common clock without seeing the name of Seth Thomas.

Of what material were Clocks made for a long time?

Entirely of wood, various kinds being used for the

different parts. In 1837, a clock having brass wheels, etc., was invented that would run for thirty hours, and in a few years eight-day clocks appeared.

Were they very expensive?

No; the expense of manufacturing them had been lessened so much, that good 30 hour clocks were sold for 75c. each, and those running 8 days for $4.

Has the business continued to increase?

Yes, very rapidly; all the parts being now made by machinery. Every year immense numbers are exported to all the countries of Europe; also, to China, Japan, and S. Africa, and many firms are busily engaged in turning out these useful articles.

Which is the leading Company?

That of Seth Thomas & Co. They make over 150,000 clocks every year. The whole number manufactured in the U. S. is about 725,000, their value in the market being at least $1,850,000.

What change has been made in the method of making Clocks?

It has been found that the "*movements*" or wheel work of a watch will answer as well for clocks, the weights and pendulum being unnecessary, although still used in the common clocks.

What are substituted for them?

The main-spring and fusee. By this change clocks can be made of almost any shape or style, so that greater variety and beauty are attained, which is a great object with both buyers and sellers.

How is the skill of the workman displayed?

Not only in the beauty of the exterior finish, but also in the curious workmanship of the parts within.

Who have shown the most skill in this matter?

The Swiss and Germans. They produce musical clocks, so made that in striking the hour a beautiful tune is played, at the same time little figures come out and dance to the music.

What has recently been made?

A very wonderful clock was produced in Europe not long since, that not only marked the hours of the day but also gave the days, weeks and months of the year, with the positions of the heavenly bodies for any time required. At a certain hour figures also appear representing our Lord and His Disciples, who go through some of the scenes recorded in the Holy Scriptures. This was all done by the curious movements of the wheel work within, being the result of much labor and skill.

CHAPTER III.

WATCHES.

Were Watches made before Clocks ?

No; clocks were first manufactured. Watches are mentioned as being made at Nuremburg, Germany, as early as 1467 by Peter Hele.

What can you say of their size?

Some were quite small, others were as large as dessert plates, many were egg-shaped and at first called the "Nuremburg Animated Egg."

Was a Watch easily made ?

By no means. At first a year was required to produce one, the price even as late as the beginning of the 16th century, being $1,500.

Was it a good time-keeper ?

No; as it was likely to vary at least an hour every day.

What change took place ?

In the course of the next hundred years some improvements were made, by which the time was more exact and the watches cheaper. But the shape was still very clumsy, being almost like a ball, and was therefore called a " *bull's eye.*"

What nation has until recently taken the lead in Watch-making ?

The Swiss, who are able to produce the article much cheaper than their rivals, the English.

How can they do so ?

Each workman makes it his business to produce one particular part of the watch, as the main-spring, fusee, barrel or some other piece. In this way he is able to do more and better work than if his skill and attention were divided among all the parts.

Do the Swiss use machinery ?

To some extent. Yet, much of the work is still done by hand, and of course is liable to many imperfections not found in machine work.

How were the principal parts of the Watch at first made?

A little cylinder called the "barrel" had the main-spring—a very fine, delicate piece of steel—coiled within it, which moved the cylinder. Around the barrel a thread of catgut was wound, which connected it with the fusee.

What is the fusee ?

It is a little grooved, cone-shaped wheel. When the watch was wound, the catgut passed on the fusee from the barrel, at the same time that the main-spring was coiled up. The last coils of the catgut were on the small end of the cone, as can easily be seen by examining a watch.

Is this method still in use?

Yes ; the same principle accomplishes the desired object, viz., to obtain great regularity in all the " movements," as the accuracy of the time-piece depends upon this.   A chain has now been substituted for the catgut.

Explain how this principle works.

When the watch is wound up, the main-spring is of course very closely coiled, and therefore unwinds at first with much more force than afterwards, so that if there was nothing to counteract this greater power, the watch would go much faster when first started than later.

Has anything been invented to accomplish this?

Yes ; a curious contrivance called the *fusee*, already described.

Explain its action.

As we have said, the main-spring uncoils at first very quickly, but at the same time the chain on the fusee unwinds and passes on around the barrel, commencing at the smaller part of the cone where, though the power is great, yet the leverage, or action of the lever, is small, so that it unwinds quite slowly, but after a little, this gradually increases unwinding faster while the movement of the main-spring has decreased in the same proportion.

How long does this variation continue?

Until the watch has " *run down*," as we say, or until all the chain from the cone has passed on to the barrel, when it must be again wound, and the same movement is continued.

With what is the fusee connected?

With the first, or principal wheel of the watch by a ratchet or a small tooth at the bottom of the fusee, which stops it while winding up, although sometimes by means of a stiff spring in the great wheel the watch is still allowed to go on.

Are the chain and fusee now used in Watches?

The English being strongly attached to their old methods of work, still use them, but they are dispensed with in the American and Swiss watches.

What advantage in that change?

The works are now very simple, as the numerous pivots and links with the chain and fusee, add about 600 pieces to the "*movements*," which, with the remaining parts, increase the number to 800 in a complete English watch. A good American time-keeper requires only 150 or 200 pieces.

What regulates the motion of American Watches?

A delicate hair-spring, which can readily be seen in an ordinary watch. By the connection of this spring with the balance-wheel, the latter performs the work of the best pendulum.

To what is it fastened?

One end is attached to the axis of the wheel, the other to the frame. The balance moves by means of a little scape-wheel, similar to the clock escapement its motion being regulated by the hair-spring.

If a Watch goes too fast or too slow how is it regulated ?

Simply by lengthening or shortening this delicate spring, on the same principle as a clock is regulated by varying the length of the pendulum.

Of what are these springs made ?

Those in general use are of the very best tempered steel.   It has been found, however, that glass answers the purpose still better, not being affected by the heat and cold, but for some reason they have not been generally introduced.   Glass has been tried successfully for balance-wheels.

How are Watches usually wound up ?

By a key placed in a hole on the cover.   Recently, however, a method has been devised by which the key is dispensed with.   Certain springs in the handle answer the same purpose.

What kind of a Watch had Napoleon I. ?

He carried one that could be wound by the motion of the body when walking.

CHAPTER IV.

AMERICAN WATCHES.

How long has the Watch-making business been carried on in this country?

It is only within a few years that the complete manufacture of watches has been conducted in the U. S.

How were they made here before that time?

The springs, fusees and escapements were all imported, for at least sixty years, and then with great trouble and labor, combined with the other movements that were worked out.

Why did not the Americans make all the parts?

They did not know how; and the Swiss were unwilling to teach them, or even allow any of their machines, models or drawings to be exported, lest they should lose the control of the business, which had been so long very profitable to them.

Were the Americans discouraged by these obstacles?

No; with determination and perseverance they found a remedy for the difficulty, as in the case of

Mr. Lowell, who invented his own machines for manu-facturing cotton cloth, already described.

Explain in what way ?

An ingenious watchmaker, A. L. Denison of Boston, conceived the idea of including in one manufactory all the machinery necessary for making every part of a perfect watch. By so doing, he thought it would be possible to turn out ten watches per day.

What had been the previous method ?

In Switzerland, where nearly all the " *movements* " were made, there were separate workmen, machines, and often a different room or building for each piece.

How did people regard the proposal of Mr. Denison ?

Many thought he was crazy, but at length he per-suaded three other watchmakers to join him, and to-gether they built a factory at Roxbury, Mass., in 1852.

Did they meet with any difficulties ?

Yes, very many ; the greatest of which was the want of plans and machines. As they could not obtain any from Switzerland, they determined to make their own.

What success had they ?

In 1853, the first watch was completed, an excellent time-keeper, although not as elegant as many have since been made.

Can you mention any other difficulty to be met ?

The workmen found that a certain fine dust, con-stantly rising from the clay soil, was injurious to the more delicate parts of their work. Consequently the establishment was removed to Charles River, near the village of Waltham.

Is it still in operation?

Yes ; and employs 700 workmen, turning out 80,000 watches every year. In 1870 they had made 500,000 since the commencement of the business.

Are there factories in other places?

Yes ; at Springfield, Mass., Newark and Marion, N. J., and at Elgin, Ills.

What can you say of the latter?

That at Elgin even rivals the Waltham factory.

How, and when was it commenced?

Some active business men in Chicago felt that watches could be made at the West, as well as in Mass., and they determined to try the experiment, which commenced in 1864.

What can you say of the undertaking?

They found it to be much greater than they had at first supposed ; still they persevered, and after spending some $500,000 in the business, the result was a complete success.

How do their watches rank for excellence?

There are none superior to them ; being considered the most accurate time-keepers known, and will stand the severest tests that may be applied to them, being used constantly on the cars and at sea, without any variation.

Although established so recently, what is the Elgin Factory able to do?

In 1870 it employed 450 hands, and produced from 40,000 to 50,000 watches annually, of nine different patterns.

Do they make the complete article?

No ; the movements only are manufactured by them. They sell these to the dealers in watches, who case them as they choose, to suit their different customers.

How does these Watches compare with the English?

They are much more simple, having only 156 pieces, being thus easily repaired, while they are also very durable and accurate.

What peculiar system is followed in making them?

In every watch of the same pattern the corresponding pieces are exactly alike, so that if any part is injured it is only necessary to send the number and style of the watch, mentioning the part that is defective, and by return mail an exact duplicate will be sent.

Is there any other peculiarity in these Watches?

They have a curiously contrived "dust-band," as it is called, which encloses the more delicate parts of the works so completely that they are perfectly protected.

How do foreigners regard these Watches?

They value them so highly that many known to be made in Europe, bear the names of Americans as manufacturers, to make them more saleable. Others in this country, who cannot make their "movements" equal to the Elgin or Waltham works, will import some of very inferior quality, and putting them together, sell them for real American watches, using the label of some well-known company or firm.

Where are the real American Watches found?

In every part of the world, the demand for them

being very great.   In this, as in many other improvements already mentioned, we are indebted to the persevering skill and ingenuity of our energetic country-
men.   For in no other nation do we find the same traits
of character so fully and generally developed as in
America.

SECTION XI.

CHAPTER I.

PLATED WARE.

What is Plated Ware ?

It is any common metal, as copper, brass, britannia, etc., upon which a thin coating of gold or silver is placed.

How is this done ?

The present method is by electro-galvanism ; but another was used for many years before this was known.

Explain the old process ?

The figure to be gilded was made of iron, brass or some base metal, as it is called. This was polished and heated until the metal became blue, then the leaf gold was applied, when it was polished a little, heated and polished again.

Was there any other method ?

Yes ; metals could be gilded by a process called *amalgamation.*

Explain it.

An amalgam is a mixture of mercury with gold, silver, and other metals. This being formed into a paste was applied to the metal by dipping or spreading it over the surface, to which it adheres. Being then exposed to heat the mercury evaporates, leaving the gold on the metal. It is then polished and the work completed. Buttons, etc., are gilded in this way.

Sometimes we see ornamental gold figures on steel: how was that done?

The gold was dissolved in nitro-muriatic acid; ether, or some volatile oil was added, when the mixture being shaken, the gold and ether unite. This was then applied to the steel in whatever figures were required with a camel's-hair brush.

What was then done?

On being exposed to heat the gold became firmly united to the steel, and could be polished. Sword-blades were ornamented in this way.

What success was attained by this method?

The work was done so well that it became difficult to distinguish the gilded from the pure gold metal, and the demand for the real article became much less.

Did this gilding ever wear off?

It would last for some time with great care; but the metal could not be re-gilded if once worn off.

How long were these methods of gilding in use?

Until 1839, when Mr. Ames, an American, was sent to England by our government to gain some information about the improved methods of making fire-arms.

To what was his attention directed while there ?

The English were then very much interested in the new method of obtaining coatings of silver by electricity. Although it had not yet been practically applied, this attracted his notice.

What resulted from the experiments made ?

An entirely new process was discovered for plating metal, called electro-plating, because the work was done by means of electricity.

What is electricity ?

This is not certainly known; like heat, we can only judge of it by the effects produced, which are more powerful than from any other natural agent known.

Has it been applied to any useful purposes ?

Yes, very many ; the most important, is the Telegraph ; a current of electricity being applied at one end of the wire, it will at once run the whole length and cause a vibration at the opposite end, and these vibrations being made of different lengths by the operator, words are indicated, and a message is sent any distance required.

Can you mention any other uses of electricity ?

It is often employed by physicians to cure certain diseases ; machines are sometimes worked by this agent ; one of the most brilliant lights is produced by it, called the electric light. It is also used with diving machines, so that persons can remain a long time under water, where it will be as light as day. It is almost indispensable for light houses.

How were metals plated by it?

When first used, a plate of zinc was suspended in a vessel containing sulphate of copper ; the object to be coated was also hung on wires .very near the zinc plate.

What followed ?

A current of electricity being sent through them, the zinc dissolved, and some of the copper was deposited on the object ; it was then said to be copper-plated. If silver was required instead of copper, the metal was first dissolved in nitric acid, distilled water and a preparation of potassium were added, the mixture being then washed, and more potassium added, could be used instead of the sulphate of copper.

What is found to be a still better method ?

A plate of silver, suspended in a solution of potassium, is connected with that part of a battery where there is most electricity, called the positive pole. As this fluid passes over to the other end, which is the negative pole, where there is not so much, it has the power of taking some of the silver and depositing it at that point.

What then takes place ?

The object to be coated is suspended by a copper wire, and dipped in nitric acid, then placed in the solution above mentioned, when silver is deposited on every part of it, taking care to keep it in motion that the whole surface may be coated alike.

Is the work now complete ?

No ; after the object has remained some time in the

solution, it is taken out and well brushed with sand. It is then placed in the mixture, and after a few hours will be found to have a coating of dead white silver, that can be polished with a hard brush and whiting, when it will come out perfectly bright.

What is the advantage of the electro-plating over the old method?

It is done much more readily and smoothly, and proves as durable as that for silver coin.

How much silver is required by this process?

To form a plate as thick as ordinary writing paper, $1\frac{1}{4}$ or $1\frac{1}{2}$ oz. of silver to 12 sq. inches.

Can ornaments be used on plated ware?

Yes ; the most beautiful and delicate designs are produced as perfectly as on the solid silver material.

CHAPTER II.

MANUFACTURE OF PLATED WARE.

Are there any manufactories for silver-plated ware in the U. S. ?

Yes ; the largest in the world is in this country, and is called " The Meridan Britannia Co.," having six large factories in different places, employing about 1000 men, making goods of 3000 different patterns, valued at nearly $2,000,000 annually.

Is the plating on their goods always of the same thickness ?

No ; this varies according to the quality required ; the thinnest coating is called single-plated, then there are the double, triple or quadruple varieties.

Mention some of the articles produced by this Company.

Knives, forks, spoons, castors, dinner, coffee and tea sets, ice-pitchers, goblets, vases, fruit-dishes, cake baskets, statuettes, and in short, every conceivable article for table or ornamental purposes.

Are any of their goods exported?

Yes ; vast quantities every year : they also produce articles not usually found elsewhere.

Mention some of them.

Porcelain-lined ice pitchers, by which the water retains its purity of taste better than if lined with metal. Also the porcelain-lined baking dish. It is an iron dish lined with porcelain. This fits into an outer plated pan, which makes an elegant and useful dish for the table. They also make forks and spoons very durable, by plating the parts most in use more heavily than the rest.

Can you mention any other company largely engaged in making silver ware?

The Gorham Manufacturing Co., of Providence, R. I. They use the electro-plating method to some extent, although it is mostly the solid silver ware that comes from their establishment.

What is the extent of their business ?

They employ about 450 hands, and use nearly 30 tons of silver every year.

Can gold be applied to metals as well as silver by electricity ?

Yes ; it is dissolved in nitro-muriatic acid, which gives chloride of gold, this is mixed and heated with powdered magnesia, then washed, by boiling in nitric acid, and afterwards dissolved in a preparation of potassium.

What follows ?

The rest of the process is similar to that described

CENTURY VASE.
Manufactured by the Gorham Company.

for plating silver. But as iron, lead and steel do not readily receive the gold plating, they are therefore first thinly coated with copper, when the precious metal can be easily applied.

Is much gold required for the process ?

No ; an ordinary watch case can be well covered within and heavily coated without, yet only 20 grains will be required, worth about $1.50. Three grains are sufficient for a handsome gold pen holder, worth only 22 cents.

Why are plated articles then so much more expensive than the little amount of silver and gold would lead us to expect ?

Because the various methods and steps required to form a perfect article from the rude materials, require much time and labor, far more valuable than the gold or silver used.

SECTION XII.

CUTLERY.

CHAPTER I.

CUTLERY IN GENERAL.

What is meant by cutlery?

This term is applied to various sharp cutting **or** pointed instruments made of iron or steel.

Of what did the ancients make such articles?

As they did not understand the use of metals, their cutlery was made of sharp stones and shells, the latter being still in use among rude and savage nations.

How did the Egyptians show their skill in this matter?

They understood the art of giving to bronze a peculiar hardness, equal to the best tempered steel, which admirably adapted it to cutlery purposes.

What is bronze?

Bronze is a metal, compounded of copper and tin, to which zinc and other metals are sometimes added, according to the purposes for which it is intended.

What did the Greeks use?

Bronze seems to have answered the same purpose with them as for the Egyptians. Homer, their greatest poet, mentions in one of his poems, called the " *Odyssey,*" the process for tempering it. The Romans also used it for swords, surgical and other cutting instruments.

How is this known?

These articles, found among the ruins of Pompeii and Herculaneum, are all of bronze.

What other nation used cutlery?

At the time the Romans, under Cæsar, invaded Great Britain, spears, hooks, broadswords, scythes, etc., were found made of iron. In later years, Sheffield was noted for its manufacture of cutlery; the reputation then gained being still preserved.

What is the principle material used in making these articles?

On account of its hardness, steel is preferred to other metals.

What is steel?

It is made from wrought iron, that from which every other material has been removed; when this is united with carbon, steel is produced.

Explain the process.

Bars of wrought iron, covered with charcoal, are placed in boxes filled with sand; these being closed, are exposed to intense heat for ten days. On opening the boxes, the iron bars are found changed into steel.

What are its peculiar properties?

It can be made either very brittle or elastic ; this is owing to the manner in which it is prepared.

Are the articles already mentioned, made entirely of steel ?

No ; the backs and handles or " *tangs*," as they are called, are usually of iron, which of course is much cheaper, the edges only being of steel.

Mention some of the different kinds of steel.

While being made, little blisters form on the surface from vessels of carbon that have burst ; this is called *blistered steel.* When it is heated, rolled, hammered, etc., many times, a much purer article is obtained, named " *shear steel,*" because it is used for shears, scissors, scythes, etc.

What is cast steel?

This is made from wrought iron or blistered steel, by being mixed with powdered charcoal, then melted, and formed into ingots, and rolled or hammered into plates, bars, cannon, etc.

What effect has hammering, rolling and heating upon this metal ?

It becomes very elastic and pliable ; the very best being used for watch springs and sword blades.

What ancient nation excelled in the manufacture of steel?

The people of Damascus ; and so successful were they in producing the famous " Damascus Blades," that all attempts to imitate them have until recently proved fruitless.

Why were these blades held in such esteem ?

On account of the many different uses that could be made of them.

Mention some.

The steel was so hard and well tempered, that its keen edge could both cut the heavy iron spears of the enemy in battle, and the thinnest gossamer fabric ever made, which cannot be done with the best English blades. It could also be rolled, bent or folded in any shape, and at once became as straight as at first.

What other peculiarity was observed in them ?

The polished surface of the blade was covered with delicate lines, some parallel, others waving and cross-ing each other, or formed in knots and bunches.

Were these marked on the steel after the blade was made ?

No; they seemed to be formed in the very sub-stance itself, though in what way is unknown.

Has the method of making the Damascus blades yet been found out ?

After repeated experiments and failures for a long time by the most skillful persons, at length, a few years ago, M. Bréant, a Frenchman, and Gen. Anos-soff, a Russian, succeeded in producing steel, having all the qualities and appearance of those of Damascus.

Were both methods alike ?

We cannot of course tell whether the process in both cases was the same or not ; that, however, makes but little difference, provided they attained the desired object.

How did they accomplish this ?

M. Bréant melted soft iron with a small proportion of lamp-black, and obtained an excellent quality of steel ; yet not equal to the Demascus. Gen. Anossoff made use of another method, which was that used in India.

Explain it.

About a pound of iron ore is placed in a crucible or clay vessel, to which are added bits of wood and straw covered with green leaves. These crucibles are then so closely protected by moistened clay, that no air can enter, and are placed, about 20 together, in a small blast furnace.

What follows ?

They are kept as hot as possible for two or three hours, and when removed, the crucibles being broken, the iron has become steel in the form of lumps.

Is it always of good quality ?

No ; usually about one-fifth of the ore is defective. This is known by the appearance of it. If the surface is smooth and marked with delicate lines, it is con-sidered excellent. But if rough and jagged, it must be rejected.

Is the operation now complete ?

No ; the best lumps are melted again, and to re-move the brittleness, they are kept red hot for some hours in a furnace, when the steel becomes soft and can be easily hammered.

By experiments made, what did Gen. Anossoff learn about the quality of steel ?

He found out that the peculiar marks which ap-peared after tempering, proved its quality.

In what way ?

If the lines were straight the steel must be bad, but if short and broken up, it was a little better, and if little lines and knots appeared, this was the best of all.

Had the color anything to do with it ?

Yes ; if little color is visible the steel is inferior, but if of a yellowish golden hue and brilliant lustre, it is considered excellent.

How many methods did Gen. A. use for making the true Damascus blades ?

There were four. Only one, however, was thought very practicable.

Explain it.

The best method was to melt the iron mixed with graphite in crucibles ; each one containing about 12 lbs.

What is graphite ?

It is a certain kind of metal used for lead-pencils.

Is any thing else added ?

Usually a little preparation of lime, so that the other substances may unite more readily. The crucible being then closely covered and placed in the fire, great heat is applied.

How long does it remain there ?

For five or six hours, when the crucible is allowed to cool ; the metal is removed in lumps, and must then be tempered, that is, heated and hammered several times to improve its quality, and when red-hot, plunged into boiling grease, and left to cool.

What follows ?

When taken out, the blade, or whatever instrument may have been formed, is wiped perfectly clean, and rubbed on one side with a whetstone. It is then heated again, hammered, and while red-hot plunged into cold water.

Is the color of the blade the same through the whole length ?

No; this varies in different parts. A sabre blade is so tempered, that the point is brought to a blue heat, which is not so great as red,—the middle, to violet— along the edge, to yellow, and near the handle, green.

Can it be ground and polished much ?

No ; this is apt to injure the quality of the metal, although with great care, a very fine and delicate edge can be given it—after which it is rubbed over with olive oil and wiped very dry—when the operation is complete.

What can you say of razors made by this process ?

They are found to be far more serviceable than those made by the English. The same is true of scythes and other articles produced at the establishment of Gen. Anossoff, at Zlatoosk, in the Ural Mts.

CHAPTER II.

KNIVES AND FORKS.

What are the most useful forms of cutlery?

Knives and forks are the most common, although other articles may be equally useful.

Have they long been used?

Probably knives in some form and of different materials have been made by all nations, from the earliest periods: but forks seem to be a modern invention.

When were they first used?

This is not certainly known. Probably not before the 13th or 14th centuries. A traveller in the time of Queen Elizabeth says, that while at Venice, he was served with a fork to hold his meat when cutting it, as the people there did not think it polite to touch it with the hand.

Can you mention a similar instance?

Another Englishman, who had travelled in the time of James I., 1608, writes to a friend, that he thought it best to adopt the Italian fashion of using a fork at his meals! Before this the fingers answered the same purpose.

How are they made?

Common steel forks are hammered, while hot, out of steel rods, each piece being of the right size for a fork. The *tang* and shank are roughly shaped at one end of the rod. About an inch of the square steel being left at the other end.

What use is made of that?

The prongs are formed of this by drawing it out perfectly flat. Being then brought to a " *white heat*," it is laid in a steel die, while in a heavy block of metal, another die is made to fall upon it from a height of 7 or 8 feet.

What is the effect of this operation?

The die cuts out two strips of steel, leaving three prongs on the fork, which are then smoothed and dressed by means of a fly-press.

What is the meaning of shank and tang?

The " tang " is the handle of the instrument, and the " shank," the blade or long part. After these have been roughly cut out, they are shaped by a die and swage. The latter being an instrument for shaping metals.

What then follows?

A number of forks are annealed by heating and cooling slowly, which makes them soft and easily shaped by filing and bending.

Is the work now complete?

No; they must be hardened. This is done by making them red hot, and then plunging into cold water, after which they are tempered.

Why is this necessary ?

As metals are applied to different purposes, the tempering depends upon the use to be made of them. If hardened without tempering, the article becomes brittle, and would easily break.

How is this effected?

The metal is heated again, and suddenly plunged in cold water. The greater the heat, the stronger, softer and more elastic the steel ; such is the material required for sword-blades, etc. But if great hardness is desired, as for axes, etc., the heat is less.

How is it known when the right temper is obtained?

The various degrees of temperature have different colors, which guide the workman, and decide the quality of the steel.

Give an example.

430° F. gives a pale-yellow, suitable for lancets ; a few degrees higher makes a deeper shade, for razors and surgical instruments. Then by gradual increase of heat, the color deepens through the shades of yellow on to purple, blue, and green, adapting the steel to pen-knives, chisels, shears, axes, table-knives, sword-blades, watch springs, small and large saws, etc. The latter requiring 610°, the greatest heat used in tempering.

Are the forks finished after being tempered?

No ; they must be ground and polished, which is one of the most unhealthy operations in the cutlery business, on account of the fine dust which fills the room, causing inflammation of the lungs.

Can this be prevented ?

If the troughs used in grinding are furnished with a ventilating fan and flue, much of the dust is carried off.

How is the grinding done ?

The process for forks, as well as other instruments, is similar, so that one explanation answers for all.

Will you give it ?

The rooms in which the grinding is done are called "*Hulls.*" Here are some six or eight troughs, as they are called. Each one includes a stone for grind-ing, a polisher, and the pulley for working it.

Are the stones of the same size?

No ; they vary from 4 inches to 2 feet in diameter. Those used for razor blades have a convex surface, which gives the concave form to the instrument.

What is the meaning of convex ?

It means *curved out ;* and concave, *curved in.* The outside of a globe is the convex part—the inside, *the concave.*

Is water used in grinding ?

Sometimes it is necessary, so that the temper of the steel may not be injured by the heat caused from *dry grinding.* If water is used, the operation is safe and healthy, although slower. Forks are always ground without water, and those who follow this business con stantly, seldom live more than 30 years.

After grinding, what follows ?

, The glazing, or *lapping*, as it is called.

How is it done ?

The " glazier " is a wooden wheel, and the " lap " of the same material, having its edge covered with a metal rim, and grooved to hold the oil and emery for dressing. The article to be smoothed is placed against each of the wheels in turn, and as they revolve, the instrument is polished.

If a higher degree of dressing is required, what must be done?

A stick of charcoal and smooth piece of flint is applied. For razors, etc., wooden wheels are used, covered with leather, and fed with dry crocus.

What is " crocus ? "

This name is given to a fine yellow dust formed from different metals.

Of what are the handles made ?

Ivory, horn, mother-of-pearl, tortoise-shell, bone, etc. ; certain kinds of wood are used for forks, knives, or various other cutting instruments.

How are they fastened?

A solid piece of the right size and shape is cut out, a hole being bored in one end for the tang, the two are then fastened together by cement or a little spring catch, contrived by Rodgers, of Sheffield, Eng.

Is there any other method ?

Yes ; sometimes the handle is bored entirely through ; at the end a little metallic cap is riveted to the tang, as may be seen by examining a knife or fork.

Are the handles of penknives fitted in the same way?

Not exactly ; as more care is necessary to do the work well. The springs for working the blades require a peculiar temper, glazing and nice fitting : the thin plates called scales, forming the sides and parts of the handle, must be exactly shaped and fitted to each other, so that it is much more difficult to produce a complete handle to a penknife, than the blade.

What can you say of a three-bladed knife?

It is said to pass through the operator's hands about 100 times before being complete.

Of what are the blades made?

The small blades are hammered out of the best cast steel. A small tang is then drawn out while hot, and fastened to a temporary handle, so as to be ground.

How are they tempered?

Several blades are placed over the fire upon a flat iron plate. When a brown or purple color appears, they are dipped in cold water, and afterwards polished.

CHAPTER III.

OTHER ARTICLES OF CUTLERY.

Are the blades of table knives made like those described in the last chapter?

The method is different. Pen-knives are formed of pure steel, but larger ones are made chiefly of iron, as being much cheaper.

Explain the process.

The blade of a table-knife is hammered out very thin upon an anvil, from a piece of shear or cast steel. This is then welded on to a bar of wrought iron, and cut off, enough of the latter being left at one end to form the tang.

What is the meaning of welded?

It is the process of uniting two metals by beating them together while very hot ; when thus joined, they appear but as one metal.

What is now done?

The blades are " smithed ;" that is heated, and hammered again, when the name of the maker is stamped upon them ; they are then hardened by heating and plunging into cold water, and being tempered to a blue color, are ready for grinding.

Of what are razors made?

The very best cast steel is used; the blade is shaped upon the anvil from a piece as thick as the back of a razor, and half an inch wide—then well "*smithed*," so as to condense the metal as much as possible. After this, one part of the blade is ground down as thin as necessary, while the back is left thick. Only the best steel will bear this operation.

What follows.

By grinding on a dry, coarse stone, the shape is improved; the stamping and drilling of a hole for the pin of the joint having been already done, it is ground on a wet stone, glazed and polished several times; the last operation being done on a soft wheel, covered with dry crocus, and turning slowly, when it is ready for the handle.

What materials are used for scissors?

They vary according to the quality of the article; the common kind are of shear steel, the blades only being tempered; while the best are entirely of the purest cast steel, all the parts being hardened.

What can you say of tailors' shears?

In these the blades only are of steel; the rest is iron. Some are made of a good quality of cast iron, called "virgin steel;" others are of an inferior kind of iron, to be exported.

What is the price of the cheapest?

A dozen are sold for about 7 cents. While those

of the best steel, having the bows and handles of gold, sell for $50.00 each.

If made wholly of steel, what is the process ?

The blade is hammered out from the end of a small bar of that metal, and cut off the required length, allowing for the shank and bow. To form the latter, a hole is punched, being enlarged by means of a small anvil.

How is the blade shaped ?

This is done by hammering and filing, the hole being bored for the screw or rivet, the blade is ground, filed smooth and polished with oil and fine emery. The ornaments are added by means of dies, which contain the patterns.

How are the blades shaped ?

They are slightly bowed so as to touch each other only at the point of cutting, and this point constantly changes as the blades close in the act of cutting, from the pivot to the point, which can be easily seen by holding a pair of scissors up to the light.

When closed, where do the blades touch each other ?

Only at the point and middle. By this arrangement greater smoothness is given to the movement of the scissors.

Are the blades made by pairs ?

No; they are formed of various sizes, and when ready to be riveted, then matched and paired.

CHAPTER IV

CUTLERY IN THE UNITED STATES.

Have the Americans paid much attention to this branch of industry?

Until recently all the cutlery in use here was imported from Europe.

What can you say of the progress lately made?

It has been very rapid ; the articles produced here far surpass those of the Old World, both in the excellence of the metals, the useful models and remarkable degree of finish given them.

What is the cause of the wonderful progress made in all useful works in this country?

It is doubtless owing to the great opportunities every intelligent, wide-awake workman has of improving in all branches of his business. But in England, a person is only instructed in a particular portion of the work, knowing little or nothing of the rest, so that an apprentice has great difficulty in becoming master of his trade.

Are the English fond of improvements?

They are so attached to their own methods, that it is difficult to introduce changes in modes of work.

How is it with the Americans?

It is just the reverse with them; they are ever on the alert, searching constantly for some better way of accomplishing their labor, so that in the case of cutlery, as in many others, the Americans have done in a few years the work of centuries in other countries.

What can you say of an apprentice in this country.

When a boy enters the factory, he is of course assigned some particular branch of the business, but while being instructed in this, he is at liberty to learn all he can from his companions, many of whom are skilful workmen, so that when he has served his time as an apprentice, he stands a fair chance to be master of his trade, and not a mere journeyman.

How long has table cutlery been manufactured in the U. S.

It was commenced in 1834, by Mr. Russell, of Greenfield, Mass. Two more factories were opened in New England, but the business seemed to make little progress at first.

What caused a change for the better?

A machine for making the blades was invented by Mr. Russell, which resulted in improvement in the business, both here and in Europe, where it was introduced. Before this the work had been done by hand.

What can you say of the establishment at Green-field?

It is very extensive. There $300,000 worth of cutlery are produced every year, being used in all parts of the U. S., as well as exported to S. America, Australia, and other countries.

Are axes made in this country?

Yes ; the largest factory in the world is in Connec-ticut. The articles produced there are shipped to vari-ous places, being considered superior to àny others.

How are they made?

The latest process forms them from hammered bar iron made red hot, and cut into pieces of the proper size. The eye which is to receive the handle is then punched through each one.

What follows?

They are heated again, and shaped by being pressed between concave dies. The edge is now grooved to receive the piece of steel that forms the cutting part. The metal is welded on at white heat, and drawn out to the right edge by trip hammers.

What is a trip-hammer?

It is a heavy iron hammer at the end of a beam, and worked by means of a wheel ; the force is very great.

What remains to be done to the axe?

It is re-shaped by hammering, and ground to form the edge ; finer stones are then used for grinding, after which it is tempered.

How is this done?

The axe is hung upon a revolving wheel over a coal

fire, and dipped first in salt, then in fresh water, and again heated in another furnace ; after this it is highly polished and stamped.   The head is blackened with a mixture of turpentine and asphaltum, which completes the work.

SECTION XIII.

PINS AND NEEDLES.

CHAPTER I.

PINS.

Have pins always been is use ?

No ; as an article of trade we do not find them mentioned until 1483.

What were used before this time ?

Persons of both sexes substituted clasps, hooks and eyes, laces with points and tags, ribbons, loop-holes, skewers of brass, silver and gold.

Do all people now have them ?

No ; savages use thorns and fish-bones for this purpose. Pins were first made of ivory, bone and silver, being much larger than those of the present day.

When was metal first applied to this purpose ?

We read of some formed of brass wire, brought to England from France, and adopted by Catharine Howard, Queen of Henry VIII. In about three years afterwards they were made in England.

What can you say of this article ?

Though so simple in appearance, it passes through many changes from the rough wire to the finished pin.

What is the first step in the process ?

Wire the size of ordinary pins is taken, and must first be straightened, which is done by winding on a reel, and then passed between 15 or 20 polished steel rollers, the last two being so close together that the wire comes out of them perfectly straight, and is wound loosely on immense spools. These are hung up until they are wanted at the machines.

How many are required to do the work ?

By a recent invention only one is necessary to form a complete pin, head, point and all, though it afterwards requires to be cleansed and polished by another process. But before this machine was invented, the method was very long and tedious, and the result far from satisfactory.

Explain the process now in use.

The wire on entering the machine, is first cut into the proper length, which of course varies with the different sizes made. The instant a piece is cut, a little hammer working so rapidly it can hardly be seen, striking the end of the wire, puts a head on it at once.

What follows ?

The wires thus headed are pushed forward sideways to a smooth plane under several " cutters," as they are called, so arranged that only the lower half of the pins come beneath them, as they are rolled swiftly to the end of the machine.

What work do these cutters perform ?

They are so arranged as to make 4000 revolutions in a minute, while pointing the pins and passing them to the receiver, where going through a spout they fall into tin vessels holding about a quart. Being examined here, the defective ones are cast aside, and the rest are put in larger pans. The pins are now complete as to their form.

What remains to be done ?

As they are covered with oil and wire filings, it is necessary to clean them.

How is this effected ?

The pins are taken to another room where there are two large revolving casks, partly filled with sawdust. A bushel or two of pins are put in, and all thoroughly shaken in order to clean them still more.

What is the next step ?

They are taken to another room, and passed through a fanning-mill, very much like that for cleaning grain. This machine being worked, the sawdust is removed, leaving the pins clean and bright.

Is the work now finished ?

Not quite ; they are taken to large tanks, in the bottom of which are blocks of tin pierced with holes. Upon these the pins are placed, then a layer of tin blocks, and so on until the tank is filled, when the whole mass is boiled by steam.

What effect is produced by this operation ?

It gives the peculiar silver color we always see, and also prevents them from rusting easily. They are now emptied into a large sink, washed, then passed again through the revolving casks and fanning-mill, when they are ready for the papers.

Is this part done by hand ?

It was formerly, when a good operative could stick five or six dozen papers in a day. But now, by an ingenious machine, one person can fill from 75 to 125 dozen a day, doing the work much more exactly than before.

Explain the working of it.

Although a large and peculiar machine, it is managed by young girls, each one sitting before the table, above which is a hopper very much like that in a flour mill, and shaken in the same way.

For what purpose are the hoppers intended ?

They contain the pins which are to be put in the papers. As the hopper moves, they fall out on an inclined iron plane, having a groove in the centre just large enough to allow all but the head of the pin to pass through.

What may be seen under this plane ?

An iron rack marked with rows of holes to correspond with those necessary to be formed in the papers. By working the machine the pins are driven evenly through the ridges on the strips of paper beneath; the process being continued until they are filled, when they can be folded and are ready for the market.

Is much time required for this operation ?

No, very little; while we are counting quickly one.

two, three, the pins have passed from the hopper, and
a row has been stuck on the paper.

*What can you say of the manufacture of pins in the
U. S.?*

Until the war of 1812 with Great Britain, they were
imported. As all commerce with England was then
interrupted, the price of pins rose so rapidly that
$1.00 per paper was charged, the quality of the article
being inferior to those now priced at six cents.

What followed?

Some Englishmen met the difficulty, by opening a
pin manufactory at the State Prison, in Greenwich
village, now a part of New York City, the convicts
being employed in the business.

How did the plan succeed?

Very well, until peace was declared, when pins were
imported so cheap that it was thought unnecessary to
make them in this country.

*Were any attempts afterwards made to manufacture
them here?*

Yes ; and many improvements also took place in
the method of making, as well as sticking them in the
papers, so that a far better article can now be produced, at two-thirds of the lowest price before paid.

*What is the extent of the business in Waterbury,
Conn.?*

One firm there has in operation a machine that will
turn out two barrels per day, or about 8,000,000 pins.

How many persons are required for the work!

The machinery is now so complete that one person

can perform the labor which formerly required thirty operatives.

How does the little American machine compare with those in other countries ?

There are none to equal it ; so that European manufacturers gladly avail themselves of the improvements it has made in the business.

16

CHAPTER II.

How long have needles been used?

Probably for centuries, as even the rudest and most savage nation had some instrument that answered the purpose, made of bone or ivory. The ancient Epyptians must have used them, as they have been found in their tombs.

Of what were these made?

They were of bronze. Pliny, a Roman, who lived more than 1800 years ago, mentions bronze needles being used in his day for sewing and knitting.

When were steel needles first used?

They were introduced into England, from Spain and Germany, in the time of Queen Elizabeth, and first manufactured in London by a German, in 1565; but the art was kept a secret until 1650, when Christopher Greening obtained the desired knowledge, and established a needle factory not far from London.

How did the needles then made compare with those of the present day?

They were very inferior in quality and finish, so

that we would now hardly be able to use what the English then considered a very fine article.

Where are most of the needles now made?

At the little village of Redditch, near Birmingham, in England. The business there is so extensive, that a large portion of Europe, the British colonies, and the U. S., are supplied with the article from that establishment.

What can you say of the process required for making a needle?

Although it seems so small and simple an instrument, yet great care and skill are necessary to make it, as it passes through many operations, and the hands of nearly 100 workmen.

Of what materials are needles made?

. The finest steel wire is generally used for the purpose, although the French take iron wire, which is changed into steel while the article is made.

What is the first step in the process?

The wire is furnished in coils of various sizes to the needle-maker. He takes those of the same quality and cuts them into pieces as long as two needles, which must now be straightened.

How is this done?

Many thousand are placed within two rings, and made red-hot. By means of a smooth file, having two grooves, in which the edges of the rings are inserted, they are rolled back and forth until the wires, rubbing against each other, become perfectly straight.

What follows ?

The wires are pointed by holding them against small grindstones that turn very rapidly, rolling the pieces all the time by a peculiar motion of the hand, now and then dipping them in cold water, that the friction may not heat them too much.

What can you say of this operation?

It proves very injurious to the health of the work-men, as few live to be 40 years old. The fine dust formed by the grinding enters the lungs, and causes a disease, named " Grinder's Asthma." Many of the workmen protect themselves by tying a handkerchief over their mouths.

What is the next step ?

The centre of each wire is flattened, and a groove made on both sides, having the place marked for the eye of the needle.

How is this formed ?

It is done by boys, who use small hand-presses for the purpose. The needles being arranged in the form of a fan are laid on an iron slab. The upper arm of the press has a couple of steel cutters or points, which are brought down and punch the eyes as each needle is brought under them.

How skilful do these boys become ?

They can punch a hole in one human hair, and thread it with another.

What next takes place ?

The needles are strung on wires, and the roughness in the eye, caused by stamping it out, is filed smooth, then the wire is divided between the two eyes, when the heads are filed into proper shape.

Is the work now complete?

No ; the needles must be hardened. This is done by placing them on iron plates made red-hot, then plunged into cold water or oil, heated again, but not so much as before, and gradually cooled.

How is it known when they are of the right temper?

The workman is guided by the color, which must be of a peculiar blue. If any are found badly shaped they are straightened by pounding with a small hammer on an anvil.

How are the needles cleaned?

They are laid in heaps upon pieces of canvas, scattering over them soft soap, oil and emery, then rolling and tying them into bundles two or three feet long, and three or four inches thick.

What are done with the bundles?

They are placed in scouring machines, that resemble mangles, and rolled back and forth for fifty or sixty hours. The friction is so great that the canvas becomes worn in about 8 hours, when a fresh piece is substituted for the old one, and more polishing materials are added. The very best needles require 7 or 8 days for scouring and cleaning.

What is next done?

The needles are placed on tin plates, when little girls are employed to turn them so that the heads shall all be one way.

Is each needle taken up separately ?

No ; by a very simple contrivance the work is done easily and quickly.

Explain it.

A piece of wash-leather is wrapped around the fore-finger, and by pressing it against the pile of needles all the points that lie in that direction are easily caught and turned the other way, and the imperfect ones removed.

What follows ?

They are placed in rows on metal plates, the eyes projecting over the edge, a piece of red-hot iron is then brought near enough to produce a sort of blue film, which shows the proper temper, when they are ready to be drilled, an operation which removes any roughness in the eye.

How is this done?

A woman takes a three-sided steel drill, and having the needles arranged in the form of a fan, causes them to be brought one by one under the action of the drill, first on one side then on the other. Much skill and a steady hand are required for this part of the work.

How are the points finished ?

They are placed upon a small revolving stone, and afterwards polished on a wheel covered with buff leather, having a coating of polishing paste.

What is the final operation ?

The needles are divided into parcels of twenty-five each, folded in colored papers, and labelled. Those to be exported are made up into packages, containing from 20,000 to 60,000 each.

Is the process just described the same for all needles?

It is for the finer qualities, but in the heavier kinds, as those used for leather work, sails, mattresses, book-binding, etc., some of the operations are omitted.

SECTION XIV

MONEY

CHAPTER I.

COINS.

What is money?

It is a medium of exchange for any articles that are bought or sold, and among civilized nations is always in the form of gold, silver or bank-notes.

From what is the word derived?

Probably from *Moneta*, the name given by the Romans to their silver coin, as it was made in the temple of Juno-Moneta.

What materials have been used for this purpose by other nations?

In the mounds near the Mississippi valley, specimens have been found made of coal, bone, shells, terra-cotta, pearl, carnelian, agate, native gold, silver, lead, iron and copper formed into different shapes, that showed more skill than the present race of Indians possess.

What do the latter use?

Their money is called *wampum*, and consists of strings of small, fresh water shells. The Carthaginians used leather, probably on the plan of our bank-notes.

What did the Chinese use?

In the 13th century some travellers from Venice visited China, and found the money there was made from the inner bark of the mulberry tree, cut into round pieces and stamped with the mark of the emperor.

Would it not be easy to counterfeit such money?

It seems so, but as death was the penalty of such a crime it was not probably often attempted.

What was formerly used in Great Britain?

There were two kinds, called "living" and "dead" money; the former consisted of slaves and cattle, which were usually sold with the land. The latter was metal.

Was money coined at first?

In the early history of ancient nations it does not appear to have been coined, but was valued according to the weight of the metal, as shekels, talents, drachmas, etc. The people of Lydia are supposed to have first coined money.

What figures were stamped upon it?

Usually those of animals: it was not until after the time of Alexander, more than 300 years B.C., that the portraits of kings and emperors were allowed to be stamped on coin. Cæsar was the first ruler to whom this privilege was granted. Gold was used in Asia

Minor for money, as it was found in abundance. But copper being more readily obtained in Italy and Sicily, bronze was substituted for gold.

What name did the Romans give their money ?

They called it "*pecunia,*" because it was often stamped with the figures of cattle, the Latin for which is "*pecus.*"

What can you say of the shape of the coin ?

It has varied among different nations. Sometimes it was in the form of rings, half-circles, diamond-shaped, etc., but among all civilized nations it is now a flat, circular piece.

What caused paper money to be first issued in this country ?

The colonists could not produce enough food and clothing for their own wants, and were obliged to buy goods from England. They soon found they had not sufficient money to pay for these things, and yet they were obliged to have them ; so paper money was used for the payment of their debts at home, which left the gold and silver for what they owed abroad.

Where is money coined ?

At a place called a mint.

Is money made at a mint for different countries ?

No ; each nation has its own. The principal one in the United States is at Philadelphia ; there are besides this five branch establishments, viz. : at New Orleans, La., Charlotte, N. C., Dahlonega, Ga., San Francisco and New York city, the last is called an

" Assay Office," the coin being tested there to prove its real value.

What else is done at the Assay Office?

At this office also the metal is received, as in the other mints, weighed, melted, refined, &c., but not coined, being sent to Philadelphia for that purpose.

When a person has gold or silver to be coined, what must he do?

He takes his " *bullion*," as it is called, to the treasurer of the mint, who weighs it in his presence, and gives him a receipt for the same.

Does this receipt show the value of the gold?

No; only its weight. The true value of it cannot be known until it has been melted and assayed, which usually requires two or three days. The person who deposited the bullion can then receive the value of it in coin, with a statement of how much silver was contained in the gold, or gold in the silver, as the two are often found mixed together. The cost of the melting, refining and coining is of course taken from the value of the deposit.

Can a mint be established, as a cotton or woollen factory, by any one who wishes to do so?

No; the coining of money is entirely under the superintendence of government, who appoint the officers and workmen. The Secretary of the Treasury has control of all the mints in the U. S.

What are the principal officers?

At each mint there is a director, treasurer, assayer,

melter and refiner, and at Philadelphia an engraver besides. The wages for those employed in the mints is paid by government, the rates being fixed by law.

What is done with the bullion to be coined?

The first step is called the "*parting process*," or separating the gold from the silver, if both are in the bullion, which is done by applying nitric acid; this dissolves the silver, leaving the gold free. By adding common salt to the solution it unites with the acid and forms chloride of silver, which can be purified by adding sulphuric acid and a preparation of zinc.

What can you say of this pure metal?

It is too soft to be used, and is therefore mixed with a certain amount of copper, making an alloy, which renders the metal hard.

What is done with this?

While melted, it is poured into moulds which, when cooled, are opened, the metal is taken out in the form of bars or ingots of the size required for coins.

What follows?

These ingots are delivered to the assayer, who tests them to prove that they are of the required quality, and then given to the treasurer, who keeps the account of their value. The ingots then pass into the hands of the coiner.

How large are they?

An ingot is a flat bar of the metal about 12 inches long, $\frac{1}{8}$ of an inch thick, and from $\frac{3}{4}$ to $1\frac{1}{2}$ inches wide, as seen in the figure.

What is done with an ingot to prepare it for coin-ing?

By means of powerful machinery worked by steam, the bars are rolled into strips of the thickness required for coin. During this process they are occasionally annealed in furnaces prepared for the purpose.

What is the next step?

The strips are made perfectly straight by being drawn through a steel gauge similar to that used for wire, and then taken to the cutting press.

How does this work?

The press consists of a steel punch fixed firmly in a mould, or round hole, of the size required for the coin. As the strips pass under this punch, the powerful machinery causes it to cut out the pieces of metal which fall into a box below. They are then carefully tested as to their weight.

Explain how this is done.

Females are employed for this part of the work. Seated before a long table, each one has a balance before her and a flat file. The gold pieces are separately tried in the scale. If the weight is too light, they are cast aside to be re-melted. If too heavy, they are carefully filed off on the edge. The "*planchets*," as they are called, are now ready for the "*milling machine.*"

What can you say of this contrivance?

It is a very simple and ingenious American invention, consisting of an upright tube in which the planchets are placed one by one, edgewise. By the revolution of two wheels the edge of each piece is crowded or pressed up into an even border or rim. They are then annealed again, cleaned and polished.

What is the last thing to be done ?

The planchets are now to be coined—that is, the required stamp for each piece of money is to be given.

How is this done ?

The coining press in use here is after the plan of the French lever machine, invented by Thonnelier. The pieces of metal are fed by hand into a tube or hopper in front of the press. A steel feeder below takes each one and passes it on to a collar, that holds it between the two dies, which make the impression on each side of it.

What follows ?

By a movement of the machine, the upper die is lifted, the feeders bring up a new planchet to be coined, which pushes away the one already stamped into the box below.

What is then done with the coins ?

They are very carefully examined by the coiner. The defective pieces being taken out, the rest are counted, put in bags, and delivered to the treasurer, when the work of making money is complete.

Might not dishonest workmen easily take some of the gold before or after it is coined ?

No ; it would be very difficult to do so. In the first place, no one is employed in a mint who has not a good reputation for honesty. Then as the bullion is so carefully weighed when brought there, the treasurer can tell almost to a penny how much coin will be made out of each piece after it is melted and purified. As the metal passes through each officer's hands, he notices carefully if the required amount is produced, and if not, the reason would be soon detected.

What is done with every person employed in the mint ?

They are all examined before leaving at night to see if they have any of the metal about them.

Is none of the gold or silver lost or wasted while being formed into money !

Of course some fine dust and small pieces become absorbed in the vessels used, or mix with the ashes, etc

Can this be obtained again ?

Yes ; by melting and burning the metal vessels and wooden tables it is procured. A recent simple invention, called a "sweep-washing machine," accomplishes the work more readily and thoroughly, preventing much of the former waste of material, so that the sweepings do not produce more than seven cents' worth of precious metal out of every pound. Formerly from 50 cents to $1 was the value obtained from the same quantity.

CHAPTER II.

PAPER MONEY.

What do we find used for money besides gold and silver?

Among civilized nations, bank-notes or paper money is often substituted for these pecious metals.

Is the paper in itself worth as much as the gold?

By no means. But, by law, it is allowed to *repre-sent* the value of as many dollars in specie as are marked upon the face of it.

Could not any one who understands how to make bank-note paper, produce as much of it as he chooses, and use it for money?

Of course not ; as that would be counterfeiting, and the laws are very severe for such an offence, although wicked persons sometimes attempt it.

How then can it be lawfully made and used?

This is the business of bankers, who are obliged to obtain the permission of government to open a bank, when it is said to be chartered.

What is a Charter?

It is a written paper, giving an individual or a company certain privileges, which they could not lawfully have without it. Every bank must have a charter before commencing business.

What is the origin of the term Bank?

The Jews were the first money-lenders of whom we have any account. They were accustomed to sit on benches or banks, as they were sometimes called, in the market-places of Italian towns, to transact their business. Hence the name Bank has since been given to all places where money is loaned or borrowed.

How many kind of banks can you mention?

There are three principal kinds, viz., Banks of Discount, Deposit and Circulation.

How do they differ?

At a Bank of Discount persons can borrow money and give in return their note, promising to pay the sum with interest at a certain time.

If the borrower should fail to do so, what is the consequence?

Then some of his property is taken as payment, or another person who signed the note with him must pay the full amount. Many who "go security," as it is called, in this way, for their friends, are obliged to sacrifice all their property, and "fail" in consequence.

What is a Bank of Deposit?

Money is put there for safe keeping, the bankers paying interest for the same. This can be drawn out at any time. If the bank should not be able to

pay out money when called for, they are said to
" suspend payment," and have, of course, failed.
This often happens.

Do the depositors then lose all their money ?

Not always.   The bankers are sometimes able to
pay a part of their debts ; usually so many cents on a
dollar.

What is a Bank of Circulation ?

This is usually combined with the other two.   The
bankers have their own paper money made, and send
it out as payment for debts.   The general law is that
when any of these bills are brought to the bank that
issues it, the holder can demand coin for the same ,
although sometimes there may be exceptions to the
rule.

Where is this paper money made ?

Usually there is a special bank-note manufactory,
that at 50 Wall street, New York city, being the principal one in this country.   There the beautiful engraving
seen on paper money is executed, each different bill
requiring peculiar marks and figures to distinguish it
from all other notes.

*Is the paper itself made like that used for other pur-
poses ?*

It varies somewhat.   The best materials are employed, and great care required, to produce a strong,
well-finished article.   A peculiar kind of shrub, growing in the marshes of the Mississippi river, is found
well adapted for the purpose.

When the engravings are stamped on the paper is the work complete?

No ; the bill must also be printed. By examining any piece of paper money you will see how much there is on each one, from 10 cents up to the largest note that is issued.

Why is it necessary to have so many different figures, words, etc., on every bill?

It is done to prevent counterfeiting ; for there are many little delicate marks that would not be noticed without very careful examination, and these are all necessary to make a "good bill."

What is the last thing to be done?

Every piece must be signed by the President--or Cashier of the bank that issues the money ; until this is done the bill is worthless. It is also numbered. This shows how many bills of that particular value have, up to that time, been issued.

By whom is the printing and engraving done?

Very honest and ˙skilful persons are employed. There is, of course, a separate press for every bill. The notes are stamped on very large sheets, each of which will produce a certain number.

How can it be known if any are taken?

An exact account is kept of every sheet that is printed. The bills being cut from it are again counted, tied in bundles of 50, 100, or more, in each, and deposited in a safe until ready to be sent to the banks for signature.

What is the result of this great care?

In making up the account of stamped bills, out of hundreds of thousands of dollars worth, the error seldom amounts to more than a few dollars, the cause of which is generally detected.

SECTION XV.

TELEGRAPHY.

CHAPTER I.

THE ELECTRIC TELEGRAPH.

What is the greatest invention ever made ?

This is a difficult question to answer. But it is generally considered that printing, the mariner's compass, steam, and the electric telegraph, have benefited mankind more than any others. Each has its own peculiar advantages, so that it is not easy to give one the preference over the rest.

What do we know regarding the latter ?

We are certain that as now used it is the greatest invention of modern times.

What is the meaning of the word telegraph ?

It is derived from two Greek words, and means, "To write afar." It includes the various methods of communicating by signals.

How was this done by the ancients ?

From the earliest times signals have been given by

means of fires kindled upon high hills, being visible by the light at night and smoke by day.

Were special, messages communicated in this way ?

They were. By previous arrangement, warnings of various kinds became known almost instantaneously for miles around.

What skill, did the Romans show in this matter ?

Their generals were able to spell out many words by using fires made of different substances.

What was the custom of the American Indians ?

They had regular stations established over our Western country for these signals. And even as recently as the time of Fremont, they used this method to give warning of his approach through their country.

Have any other, signals been used ?

Various ingenious methods have been contrived to communicate readily between places at a distance. Many of these were operated by the use of different pieces of wood, each of which represented a letter or word. The message being thus made known from some elevated point, was repeated at the next station, and thus sent on through the whole line.

How are telegraphic communications made at sea ?

Flags of various colors have long been used, each of whch indicates a word or sentence. By naval signals, 400 different sentences can be communicated from ship to ship by varying the combination of two revolving crosses.

What was the great objection to all these methods ?

They could only be used in elevated places and within certain limits.

Had the idea of telegraphing by means of electricity ever been conceived before it was finally brought into use?

It had to some extent, and experiments were made to that effect. Although it was known in 1729 that a shock of electricity could be sent some distance through conducting wires very rapidly, yet it was not until later, that any practical tests were made of it.

Why was this ?

Because the attention of persons seemed at first directed to the more visible effects of electricity produced by the Leyden jar—an invention which revealed that wonderful agent—such as communicating a shock to several persons at once, setting fire to alcohol by a charge through wires under water, etc.

By whom was this done ?

By Franklin, in 1748, across the Schuylkill river. He also proved, about the same time, that lightning and electricity were identical.

How was the electricity then produced ?

It was developed by friction, and with each discharge from the jar, ceased to act until another was produced, so that it was not then adapted for making signals, as a constant current is required to accomplish this.

What is a Leyden jar ?

It is a glass vessel, coated within and without, for about two-thirds of its depth, with tin-foil.

Why is the upper part left free?

So that the electric fluid may not be conducted from one side to the other. Through the cover a metallic rod passes, until it reaches the inner coating, and rises two or three inches above the jar. The electricity is carried along this rod, while the outer coating communicates with the ground.

How may the quantity of this fluid be increased?

By connecting several Leyden jars together, when all act as if they formed but one. This combination is called an *electrical battery*.

What invention opened the way for the present electric telegraph?

It was the discovery of the Voltaic Pile in 1800.

Will you describe it?

This is formed by placing plates of copper and zinc alternately above each other, separating each pair by a piece of paper or cloth moistened with salt or acid water.

Should the pile end with the same metal as that with which it commenced?

No; if it began with copper, the pile must terminate with zinc, otherwise copper must be at the top.

Can any other metals be used besides those just mentioned?

The same result may be attained on condition that one of the metals will be more easily oxidated or dissolved in an acid than the other. Thus copper and silver may be used, also silver and gold, or silver and platina.

What is the object of the voltaic pile?

By means of it a greater quantity of electricity can be obtained and used for a longer time than from the Leyden jar.

What simple experiment proves that electricity can be produced in this way?

If a silver dollar is placed on the tongue, and a piece of zinc beneath it, the two edges being made to touch each other, electricity will pass from the zinc to the silver.

How is this known?

The person will perceive it by a peculiar metallic taste, also a slight flash of light may be seen, either in a dark room or with the eyes nearly closed.

When was the voltaic pile applied to telegraphing?

In 1809 it was used in connection with an ingenious machine, and messages could be sent by it for a distance of at least 3,000 feet.

What objection to its use?

Sufficient electricity could not be obtained for communications at a great distance, without using an inconvenient number of plates.

What was the next step towards a successful result?

The discovery of the principles of electro-magnetism, made by Oersted, of Copenhagen, in 1819 ; but the difficulty still seemed to be to obtain sufficient power in the electricity to make it work equally at any distance.

What discovery was made a few years later?

Prof. Henry, of Albany, after many experiments

made in 1828 and 1830, proved that any amount of electricity could be obtained and used for the greatest distance required.

Explain the method to be followed?

An iron bar, either straight or bent in the form of the letter U, was wound around with many layers of covered wire, then applying it to the battery, and dipping the ends of each wire in a cup of mercury, and the two poles of the battery in the same, great magnetic force was acquired, sufficient for all telegraphic purposes.

Was the whole science of telegraphing now complete?

No; the principle was known, but great ingenuity was still required to apply it successfully.

What lesson may we learn from this?

We learn that great inventions are not made suddenly, by chance or mere good fortune; they are the result of patient, persevering thought and experiment. Also that one person alone seldom brings them to perfection.

What then is necessary?

One man may have an idea of a new invention, and bring it out in a rough, unfinished form. Another person will make some improvements in it; a third still more, until at last, after many experiments by different men, the work is brought to perfection. Almost every thing we see made by art proves this, as we have already learned in different parts of this book.

*Who was the first person to apply the electric princi-
ple, as just described, to telegraphing?*

This honor is due to Baron Schilling, of St. Petersburg.

In what way was it done?

He used for this purpose magnetic needles, each of
which corresponded to a letter or figure. As the electric current passed through a wire near these needles,
their position was changed; each needle had its own
wire covered with silk to prevent the electricity passing into other substances.

What improvement did the Baron make in this?

He gradually diminished the number of needles
until there was but one.

What happened at this time?

Schilling died, and it is not known how far his invention succeeded; but it prepared the way for greater
progress in the science of electricity.

When was the first telegraph really established?

It was made in 1836, being invented by Prof. Stein-
heil, of Munich, and adopted the next year by the government of Bavaria.

What was its extent?

It was 12 miles in length, and used but one wire.

How were the signals given?

They were made by bells of different tones, which
could be soon understood by the operator. At the
same time the bells sounded, lines and dots, to indicate
letters, were marked on a slip of paper, similar to the
plan adopted by Prof. Morse, the American inventor.

What happened the next year?

In 1837 several telegraphs were produced in different countries by various inventors, but that of Prof. S. F. B. Morse has been generally considered the most simple and useful.

Where was it first exhibited?

At the University of New York, in 1837. For five years previous Prof. Morse had made many experiments before it was brought into working condition, and for three years after this time he was still adding improvements.

When did he obtain a patent for his invention?

In 1840 ; but it was not until May 27, 1844, that it was practically used. The first message was sent from Washington to Baltimore, causing, of course, great interest and excitement.

What was first used for this purpose?

An insulated wire, that is, one covered with silk or cotton thread. This was buried in a lead pipe under ground, but as this failed, another was placed on posts and substituted for it, which answered the end proposed,

How was the electricity obtained?

It was furnished by a galvanic battery, and communicated through the telegraph wire to the electro-magnet at the receiving station.

What took place there?

A pen or pencil, connected with the magnet, made the dots or marks upon a moving slip of paper when the electricity was excited. A sharp point was afterwards used instead of the pencil. The paper is moved regularly by clock-work.

Why was this method preferred to others ?

Because but one wire was used, and the plan of lines and dots for letters, figures and signs was the simplest that had then been invented.

Is the recording instrument now generally used by the Morse telegraph ?

In many places it is dispensed with. The operator trusts entirely to the peculiar clicking sound made by the instrument, which guides him in receiving the message.

What advantage in this ?

It saves the expense of an extra assistant to read the dispatch to the copyist as it is received. The operator now writes it down as he hears the sounds.

Are not more mistakes made in this way ?

No ; it has been found that fewer errors are committed than by the former method of reading from the dotted paper.

CHAPTER II.

TELEGRAPHIC INSTRUMENTS.

You said the electricity was obtained from a galvanic battery. Will you describe it?

There are different kinds of batteries, but the general principle in all is the same. That used for telegraphing is called Groves' Battery, and is a very powerful instrument.

How is it made?

It consists of several cups, or cells, joined together. Each is formed of a cylinder of zinc, coated with mercury. Within this is a cup of unglazed clay. Both are placed in a glass cup.

How are they joined together?

A piece of zinc passes from one cup to the next, and serves to carry the electricity. A strip of plating also passes from the zinc cups, and dips into the inner one of clay.

How is the battery prepared for use, or charged, as it is called?

This is done by filling the clay cup with nitric

acid, while sulphuric acid, diluted with water, fills the space between the two cups.

Will you explain on what principle the electricity is produced by this battery?

We have before stated that if two different metals have some wet cloth or paper between them, when the two edges meet the electricity will pass from one to the other. This is exactly what takes place in the case of the battery described.

What is the object of the acids used?

As they act upon the metals of the cups, the electricity is excited, and passes in a continual circuit from the positive to the negative, and from the negative to the positive poles of the battery, and will continue to do this, if the different plates are connected, for a long time.

What are positive and negative poles?

The ends of the wires connecting the two metals are called the poles of the battery. That which comes from the wire most powerfully acted upon is called the positive, and the other the negative pole.

Is there electricity in everything?

All things in nature possess it, but in different degrees. Those giving out or manifesting the greatest quantity are called positive, and such as produce but little electricity when excited are called negative electrics.

Give some example.

It has been found that oxygen, chlorine and iodine, and generally all the acids, possess negative electricity ; while hydrogen, the metals and alkalies, are naturally positive.

What are some of the effects produced by electricity?

It gives out sparks and very brilliant flashes of light ; causes gunpowder to explode, will fuse metals, decompose water—that is, separate it into the gases of which it is composed.

How can the brightest artificial light be produced?

By putting pieces of charcoal on the wires of a powerful battery and bringing them together.

Is there much heat with the light?

The greatest heat ever obtained by man comes from the galvanic battery, which is known by the effects produced.

Mention some of them.

The metals are easily melted. Slate, lime, sulphur, magnesia and quartz are turned to liquids ; and diamond, the hardest of precious stones, melts, boils, and is changed into coal.

What kind of wire is used on telegraphic lines?

Iron wire is found to be the most serviceable. Copper, however, is a better conductor of the electricity, but is so liable to break, besides being easily affected by the temperature, that it is seldom used, except on important lines under water.

How are the wires laid in Europe and Asia?

In some cases they are buried in the ground instead of being supported on posts.

How are they prepared for this purpose?

The wire is insulated, that is, covered, so as to prevent the electric fluid from passing into other substances, by a coating of gutta-percha, then laid in pipes of lead or clay, or in wooden boxes preserved by saturating the wood with sulphate of copper or chloride of zinc.

What can you say of this plan?

Some have worked well for years, but when they fail it is very difficult, as well as expensive, to find the defective places.

How are the wires insulated when raised on posts?

Various methods have been adopted. A very excellent one is that of a glass cup fitting over the wooden pin. A cover of wood saturated, like the pin, with coal tar and pitch, is placed over the glass, entirely covering it, so that it is always dry and the wire is perfectly insulated.

What has since been used instead of glass?

In the Northern States hard rubber insulators have been very successfully applied.

How are the wires laid on the posts?

In forests they pass loosely through the supports, so that if a tree should fall upon them they may not be broken—but in open places the wire is fastened to each post.

Are the telegraphic lines easily laid?

No; great care and labor are required. The land must first be surveyed, so as to find the shortest distance between the stations. The ground is then examined, that a firm foundation for the posts may be secured. As in building railroads, these and other

points are always observed.   The telegraphic wires
are frequently erected on the railway lines.

How near each other are the posts placed?

They are from 50 to 100 feet apart, and about 20
feet from the ground.

How rapidly does the electric current travel?

From experiments it appears to be about 15,400
miles per second.

Over how many miles does the telegraphic line pass?

It is difficult to estimate exactly, as additions are
being constantly made.   In 1860 there were over
50,000 miles in operation.

How was this increased?

The next year a great addition was made by the
completion of the line from St. Louis to San Francisco,
thence to Oregon, which was opened Oct. 25, 1861.

*How do the lines in other countries compare with
those in America?*

Thus far the United States takes the lead.   Besides the European countries, we find the telegraph
in Australia, Asiatic Turkey, India, China and Japan.

What have the Russians attempted?

They proposed extending a very important line
from Moscow to the Pacific Ocean.   This will con-
nect Eastern Asia with the countries of Europe, and
Behring's Straits with the American Continent.   The
work has not yet commenced.

*Where is the principal department for telegraph
business in this country?*

It is located in a very large building in New York

city. A great many lines meet here, and extend over different parts of the U. S.

Will you describe this establishment ?

The basement serves as a store-room, where all the instruments and materials used on the lines are kept on hand, to be ready when needed.

What is done on the first floor ?

This department is for the reception of messages. In the rear is the operating room of the American division, containing 25 instruments, each arranged on its own table. The wires from the different lines enter in the rear of the room and pass on to a *"switch."*

What is the object of the switch ?

It is so arranged that any instrument in the room may be instantly placed in connection with either of the lines entering the office by means of wires that pass from the *"switch"* to each instrument.

What are found in the second and third stories ?

The second is occupied by the officers of the company, and the third serves as the operating rooms of the New York, Erie & Buffalo lines. The rooms for the Associated Newspaper Companies are on the fourth floor.

For what is the fifth story reserved ?

This is the battery room. Here are nearly 400 cups of Grove's battery, which supply all the lines with the electric current.

What other applications of the telegraph have been made in different places ?

It is used in a system of fire alarms, and so con-

nected with the bells that they can strike at the first
signal the number of the district and station where
the fire is discovered. It also indicates the exact
noon by a single stroke upon the bell of the Old
South Church, the oldest building of its kind in Boston.

What is the arrangement in London ?

By a current of electricity from the Royal Observatory, a large ball is made to drop exactly at noon,
from a pole erected in the Strand. The same thing
takes place from Nelson's Monument, in Edinburgh.
In Paris, a cannon is fired upon a similar plan.

Can you mention any other uses made of it ?

Private telegraphs are often found in large establishments, communicating from the work-shops to the
offices, and between the halls of legislation and printing rooms, so that speeches and important reports can
be printed, even while delivered.

*What is one of the most recent improvements in tele-
graphing ?*

Last year, 1875, M. La Cour, the assistant Director
of the Copenhagen Physical Observatory, laid before
the Telegraphic Conference, at St. Petersburg, a new
invention in this wonderful science.

Explain it.

He proved that it was possible to send several messages at one time, by a single wire, between two stations, so that one would not interfere with the others.

How was he led to this discovery ?

While making experiments in electricity, he found

that the current was transmitted from place to place by means of waves, similar to those of sound.

What followed ?

He arranged a series of tuning forks, each pitched to a certain note, and connected with electro-magnets, so that when a particular current passes through one of the tuning forks, it will not interfere with other currents sent through differently tuned forks, all of which are transmitted by the same wire.

Has it been adopted to any extent?

Yes ; it is in daily use on many lines in this country and elsewhere, and is called the duplex system.

When we speak of a current of electricity sent along the Line, what do we mean ?.

The word *current* is used as the most convenient term to express the action of electricity. But in reality there is nothing whatever passing along the wire. As we have said, it is merely by waves that electricity is transmitted.

Will you illustrate this?

Thus, if by the action of the electrical machine, a wave is put in motion at Boston, the power of the fluid is such, that all the intervening waves between that city and the station where the message is received, are instantaneously moved. This vibration being perceived, indicates the "*passage of the current,*" as it is called.

CHAPTER III.

SUB-MARINE TELEGRAPH.

What is a sub-marine telegraph?

It is a telegraph under the water.

When was such an undertaking first proposed?

In 1797, Don Francisco Salva projected a telegraph between Barcelona and Palma, in the island of Majorca, but probably with little success, as we do not hear of such an attempt again until 1839.

What was then done?

Experiments were made in India, by Dr. O'Shaughnessy, who insulated his wires by covering them with tarred yarn, which he enclosed in split rattan, and again covered this with tarred yarn.

What attempt was made by Prof. Morse?

In Oct., 1842, he laid a copper wire insulated by a covering of hempen thread, coated with pitch-tar and India rubber, between Governor's Island and the Battery, New York.

Did it prove a success?

Communications began to be received the day after

the wire was laid, but unfortunately it became entangled in the anchor of a vessel getting under weigh, a large part of which was taken by the sailors on board.

When was another attempt made ?

The next year, Samuel Colt laid a sub-marine cable from Coney and Fire Islands to the harbor of New York, which was successfully operated.

How was it made ?

It was coated with a preparation of cotton, beeswax and asphaltum, the whole being enclosed in a lead pipe. Mr. Colt also laid another cable from the Merchants' Exchange to the mouth of the harbor, which proved both useful and successful.

When was gutta-percha first employed as a coating for the cable ?

It was probably first applied in laying the telegraph wire across the Rhine, from Dentz to Cologne, the distance being only half a mile.

What is the greatest attempt ever made in this department of science ?

That of connecting the Old World with the New, by a cable spanning the Atlantic Ocean, which was commenced in 1857, and completed Aug. 5, 1858.

To whom are we indebted for this undertaking ?

This honor is due to Cyrus W. Field. His success was achieved only after making many experiments, and overcoming great difficulties.

What led him to think the work could be accomplished ?

Various experiments had been successfully made in

1856, by sending distinct signals through connected coils of wire, coated with gutta-percha ; the length being over 2,000 miles.

Was the result the same when the cable was placed under water ?

No ; a great difference was experienced. That which at first was a simple and constant conductor of electricity, became, when submerged, of the nature of a Leyden jar, which we have already described.

How did the cable resemble the jar?

The gutta percha corresponded to the glass, the inner wire to the interior coating, and the iron covering of the wire to the outer surface of the jar.

What was it then found necessary to do ?

The cable must be charged through its whole length before any effect could be perceived.

When the first Atlantic cable was put in operation, what was the result ?

The current was found to be so weak, that with great difficulty the signals were perceived, when sent from Valentia, in Ireland, to Newfoundland.

What may have been the cause of this ?

It was partling owing to a defect in the cable near the shore of Ireland, which was injured by handling and exposure to the sun, as well as in laying it.

How many messages were sent ?

From Aug. 13th to Sept. 1st., 129 messages passed from Valentia to Newfoundland, and from Aug. 10th, 271 in the other direction.

Were the signals given as rapidly then as now ?

No ; for the message sent by Queen Victoria to the President of the United States, consisting of 99 words, occupied 67 minutes in its transmission. The length of time required for a despatch often varied, and being frequently unintelligible required to be repeated many times.

When it was found the cable would not work, what was done ?

Every effort was made to ascertain the cause of the defect. Skilful and learned men, with powerful batteries, were employed for this purpose.

What was the result of their efforts ?

They proved that the defect must be in the cable, within 300 miles of Valentia, but that the wire had not parted in any place, as imperfect signals were still received, and therefore concluded that the fault was in the cable itself, and that it had been injured in some way.

Could the defect be remedied ?

This was impossible, as the cable would break if raised from so great a depth in the water ; it was therefore necessary to abandon this great undertaking, which caused much disappointment, especially to those who had invested large sums of money in it.

What was the cost of the first Atlantic cable ?

It was estimated at $1,834,500.

How are sub-marine cables made ?

A very common method at first adopted, and still in use, was to have a conducting wire pass through the centre, this being formed of copper wires twisted together so as to make the whole very firm and strong.

How was this insulated?

By using "Chatterston's Composition," as it is called, which consists of a mixture of gutta-percha, wood-tar and resin.

Why was this preferred to gutta-percha alone?

Because it would adhere firmly to the wires, while gutta-percha, as well as other substances, soon peeled off.

What was used besides the " Composition"?

Over a thick covering of this material were placed several layers of hardened caoutchouc alone, or alternating with the "Composition" above mentioned.

How was the cable protected from blows and accidents?

It was covered with tarred hemp, then with many steel wires, thus completing the work.

Can you mention any other method adopted?

A more simple plan is now followed. The conductor is made of a single wire cable, formed of fine smaller wires, so twisted together that if one should break the communication is not thereby interrupted.

What can you say of its weight?

This is found to be very heavy. Recently a cable much lighter has been made, but it seems to be sooner corroded by the action of the sea.

Is the cable complete on leaving the factory?

No; only the conductor with the insulators are

made there.   The outer coverings of hemp and steel are added at the port of embarkation.

What is done while the cable is being made ?

It must be constantly tested, to see if the electric current works without interruption.   Should there be any irregularity it proves that the insulating covering has broken, and the electricity is passing through an aperture into the outer wires.

How is the defect remedied ?

By cutting the metal covering and joining the broken part.   When completed, the cable is tested through its entire length ; an operation which requires great skill and care.

What was done before laying the first Atlantic cable ?

The bottom of the ocean was thoroughly examined to find out the best route.   The result proved that from Newfoundland to Ireland there was an almost level bank, as if Nature has prepared it expressly for the purpose.   The cable was laid upon this bank, which has since been called the " Telegraphic Plateau."

How was the work done ?

Two large vessels, one from the U. S., called the " Niagara," and the other from Ireland, the " Agamemnon," were to carry the cable, each having half of it.   Both vessels sailed from their ports at the same time, so as to meet in mid-ocean, where the wire could be joined.

Was not the weight of it very great ?

Yes ; that of the one we are describing averaged

about 2,200 lbs. to the mile ; but this formed, of course, the only cargo of the vessel. To make up for this ballast, as it was paid out, an equal weight of water replaced it.

How is the cable laid ?

It is packed in the hold of the vessel, being rolled upon cylinders. When the work begins, the wire passes over two very strong cast-iron wheels, turning three times around them ; from these it is carefully paid out into the ocean by passing over an iron roller placed at the stern of the vessel.

What regulates the movement of the cable ?

There are powerful brakes, or checks, which prevent the wire from passing out very rapidly. To avoid too much heat from friction, twenty men are constantly employed in pouring water on the wheels and brakes.

If the cable is not laid regularly, what is the result ?

Much trouble follows : for should it pass out too quickly, it will become tangled and knotted in the sea, and if too slowly, the strain upon the part already laid will be so great that the cable breaks. The tossing of the vessel, as well as winds and waves, add much to the difficulty experienced in the work.

Is there any communication between the ship and land during the operation ?

Yes ; constant signals pass and re-pass, proving if the cable continues in working condition.

How are the ends of the cable united in mid-ocean ?

The outer wires are laid back, while the copper

ones of each end are firmly twisted and soldered together. Being placed in an iron box, a quantity of melted gutta-percha is poured over the parts united. The box is then closely sealed and soldered, when it can be let down into the bed of the ocean.

Why are other vessels sent with the one that carries the cable ?

They accompany the ship to direct her course. As the needle of the compass is so easily affected by the electric current, it would not indicate her true position, and must, therefore, be carried by the attending vessels.

After the failure of the first Atlantic cable, was another attempt made ?

Not immediately ; as it was difficult to find persons who would risk their money in such an uncertain and expensive enterprise. Learned men, however, were carefully studying the science of electro-magnetism, that the next application of it to telegraphing might prove a success.

What was the result ?

Another cable was made, and, in July, 1865, a steamship, " The Great Eastern," was chartered to lay the whole of it

Did this prove a success ?

At first the work progressed very well, but at length violent storms arose, tossing the monster ship like a feather, and seriously injuring the work. Although the attending ships did all in their power to aid the vessel, the strain upon the cable was too great, and it parted, sinking into the bed of the ocean.

What followed ?

Notwithstanding the failure of the second enterprise, a third attempt was made, and, in July, 1866, the "Great Eastern" was again employed to carry on the work.

What was the result ?

The weather being very favorable, the cable was successfully laid, causing great joy throughout the world.

Was the second cable ever found ?

Yes; as the "Great Eastern" returned to England, she succeeded in fishing it up from the bed of the sea, united the broken parts, and completed the work of laying it.

Are these the only telegraphic lines between America and Europe ?

A third cable has since been laid by the French nation. The Emperor Napoleon used it first, sending his congratulations to President Grant. Two more have since been added.

Is it probable that electricity can be applied to any other purposes than those now in use ? ·

There are doubtless many other ways of applying it, as new methods are being constantly discovered. Attempts are now being made to substitute it for steam in the working of machinery, etc. Should success follow these efforts, wonders in science and art will doubtless be revealed, of which we have never dreamed.

What objection to this plan?

The materials for producing electricity are so much more expensive than water and coal, by which steam is generated, that economy, the chief point to be considered, would give the preference to steam, other things being equal.

What method has been recently devised in connection with this science?

The "Quadruplex System," as it is called, has been put in operation, within a few months, on the Western Union Telegraph Co.'s lines, by which four messages can be sent over a single wire at the same time.

Can you mention any other?

By the "Telephone System" music is transmitted by telegraph: and it is confidently expected that eight or more messages may be sent simultaneously by this method.

What machines are now run by electricity?

Sewing machines, small lathes, organs, and others by which very light work is done.

CHAPTER IV.

THE TELEPHONE.

What other great invention can you mention ?
The telephone.
What is the meaning of the word ?
It means " To speak from far."
When was it invented ?
It was given to the public in 1877, being previously exhibited at our Centennial.
Who was the inventor ?
The merit of this wonderful invention is probably due to Elisha Gray, of Chicago, although another American, A. G. Bell, who has made many improvements in it, also claims the honor.
How is it made ?
There are many different instruments called Telephones, all on the same general principle.
Will you describe one ?
It consists of a trumpet-shaped tube, containing a very delicate membrane, resembling the drum of the ear.

Of what use is this membrane ?

The human voice, or any sound falling upon it, causes vibrations, which are carried by two wires connected with it to an instrument at the other end, exactly like the one already described.

Of what use is this second instrument ?

It is the receiver, and is held to the ear by the person to whom a message is sent.

Can a telephone both send and receive the same sound ?

The one invented by Mr. Gray was only a transmitter, but Mr. Bell improved it, so that one instrument will answer both purposes.

What is also added to complete this Telephone ?

A piece of wire is coiled around a bar of soft iron, which has been magnetized ; through this a current of electricity is passed, causing the wire to carry the message sent.

What is this called ?

It is called an electro-magnet.

What may be heard by the Telephone ?

The words uttered at one end of the instrument may be heard as distinctly at the other as if the person were seated by your side.

Can any other sounds be sent by the Telephone ?

Yes ; both vocal and instrumental music.

Is the one just described generally in use ?

It is frequently used ; but many recent improvements have been made, by which the instrument is more simple in form, and at the same time more powerful in its effects.

To whom are we indebted for these improvements?
To Mr. Thomas A. Edison, of Menlo Park, N. J. *

* For the encouragement of young students we give a little sketch of Mr. Edison's early life, condensed from the "*Popular Science Monthly.*" Thomas A. Edison was born in Ohio, in 1847. He had the misfortune to lose his mother when 15 years old. She was a very gifted and highly educated lady, and gave her son all the instruction he ever received While still quite young he began to earn his own living as train-boy, hiring two or three other boys as assistants, which gave him more leisure to gratify his taste for reading. Some works upon chemistry having fallen in his hands, he became much interested in the subject, and procured a few chemicals, with which he made experiments; some of them were quite successful. He attempted a telegraphic instrument, using for this purpose some wire from the stove, wrapped with rags. Having no battery, he tried to obtain the electricity he needed from the cat's back; but as there was not sufficient for the purpose, he was obliged to give up the attempt. A fortunate incident soon gave him the opportunity of becoming a telegraph operator. While still a train-boy, as the cars were one day coming into a small station, he noticed a small boy, about two years old, crawling upon the track. He sprang forward just in time to rescue the child, whose father was the station-master. Being quite poor he could only reward young Thomas for his bravery by teaching him telegraphing. Therefore, every night after the day's work was finished on the train, Thomas gladly went down for his lessons, and in a short time became an expert operator, being soon employed in various offices. Although very skilful in his new employment, he spent much of his time in making experiments, chiefly connected with electricity. Having not only improved old methods of using this subtle fluid, we also find him inventing new instruments, which have become the wonder of the civilized world. Although only 31 years of age, he prob-

How was he led to make so many improvements in the Telephone?

By constant study and many experiments.

Will you give an account of one of his attempts ?

Mr. Edison had tried for a long time to find a sub-stitute so sensitive and elastic that it would be easily affected by a current of electricity passing over it, and yield to the slightest pressure.

Did he succeed at first?

No, he did not ; having tried every chemical in his shop, of which he had some 2,000.

What followed?

He did not like to give up the attempt, and while still looking for something that would answer the purpose, his assistant brought in a piece of a lamp-chimney, to which adhered a little lamp-black.

Did this prove of any use?

Yes ; the lamp-black was scraped off, pressed into a cake and placed between two metal plates, one of which was large enough to receive the sound now uttered before it.

What were attached to these plates ?

The opposite poles of the battery were fastened to these plates, so that the current of electricity passing over the cake of carbon or lamp-black, caused it to yield to the slightest pressure.

ably stands at the head of the list of living inventors. Nearly every week brings us the account of some new and wonderful machine, as the result of his great industry and ingenuity.

Will you describe another form of the Telephone in which the principles of the carbon cake is used?

This instrument, which is one of the most recent inventions of Mr. Edison, consists of a box about 10 inches wide, 18 long, and 7 deep, open at one end. A small glass tube is fastened to the top of it by sealing, wax.

What are placed in the tube?

The tube is filled with pieces of willow charcoal that have been metallized with iron.

How is charcoal metallized?

Small sticks of charcoal are placed in an iron box, having a loose cover, and gradually brought to a white heat.

Why are they thus heated?

They are heated so that any water in the pores of the charcoal may be expelled, this being replaced by vapor of iron, which, being heavier than the vapor from the water, does not pass out of the box.

What is the result?

When cooled, the sticks of charcoal are loaded with iron, and then said to be metallized.

To what use is it now applied?

Small pieces of the metallized charcoal are placed in the glass tube, as we have before said, and pressed closely together, until a portion projects from each end.

What is then done?

The wires always used in the telephone are wound around these projecting ends, and the glass tube closed with sealing-wax, when the instrument is complete.

What effect will it produce?

On holding an ordinary electro-magnet telephone to the ear, with a battery attached, the mere rubbing of the finger, or the tracing of a pencil on the box, or a house-fly walking over it, can be distinctly heard.

How is this done?

The charcoal tube being so very sensitive to the least impressions, the mere vibrations caused by the movements just mentioned will produce these wonderful effects.

What more can you tell me of this Telephone?

By means of it sounds become audible that could not otherwise be heard.

Give an example.

If a watch is placed on the box the slightest movements of the delicate works within can be heard, even to the grinding of the wheels as they pass each other, also the ring of the main-spring. If words in a low tone are uttered in the box, they will sound like the loudest trumpet; and the blowing of the breath, as the roar of the wind in a forest.

To what other practical uses can so delicate an instrument be applied?

Physicians will find it useful in sounding the lungs, heart, etc., of their patients.

How is this done?

As it is so very sensitive, the least irregularity in the pulse, heart, lungs or any other organ can be more readily detected than by any other means.

What name is given to this instrument?

It is called " The Carbon Telephone."

CHAPTER V.

THE PHONOGRAPH.

What still more wonderful instrument has Mr. Edison invented ?

The Phonograph.

What may it be called ?

The " *Child of the Telephone*," because its invention depended upon first seeing what the Telephone could do.

Will you describe it ?

It is very simple in form, consisting of a brass grooved cylinder, through which passes a long screw. At the end of this is a crank for turning the Phonograph.

With what is the cylinder covered?

It is wrapped around with tin-foil to receive the permanent impressions made upon it.

How is the instrument used ?

When a person speaks through the mouth-piece fastened to the cylinder, at each vibration caused by the voice the diamond-tipped point attached to a spring dots the tin-foil wrapped around the cylinder, reverberating the sound back again to the listener.

What makes this simple instrument so wonderful ?

That which makes it so wonderful is the fact that the impressions once made on the tin-foil, being permanent as we have said, the sounds which produced them can be heard at any time again, by simply turning the crank.

If the handle is turned backward, what is the result ?

The sentence that was uttered will be reversed, or in other words, the machine will talk backward.

What still more wonderful effect can be produced by the Phonograph ?

If a song is registered, and afterwards a speech or conversation, on turning the crank, the two utterances can be heard at the same time, and yet each will be clearly distinguishable.

How can the sound he magnified ?

A cone-shaped resonator is attached to the speaking orifice.

Is the Phonograph now complete?

By no means ; the great inventor is constantly making improvements in it ; and says he hopes yet to make it speak so loudly as to be used on board ships to warn vessels in time of fogs or any other danger.

Has Mr. Edison invented other instruments ?

Yes ; a great many.

Mention some of them.

The Aerophone, Megaphone, Microphone, Tasime-ter, etc.

What is the object of the Megaphone ?

The Megaphone is intended as a substitute for the

ear and speaking-trumpet.   Sounds being heard by it
at a great distance.

*Have any other instruments of the kind been in-
vented?*

Speaking and ear trumpets have been long in use.
One writer mentions a gigantic speaking-trumpet,
called " The Horn of Alexander."

Was it very powerful?

It is said that Alexander the Great used it to call
his soldiers at a distance of ten miles.   We are not
certain, however, that this is true, as it is generally
supposed the speaking-trumpet was invented by
Samuel Moreland, in 1670.

Will you describe the Megaphone?

It consists of three paper or pasteboard funnels,
placed side by side—the middle one, which is smaller
than the others, being used as the speaking-trumpet.

What is the size of the outer funnels?

They are about 6 feet 8 inches long and 2 feet $3\frac{1}{2}$
inches in diameter at the larger end, being used as
ear trumpets.

How far can sounds be heard by the Megaphone?

Both ordinary conversation and singing can be
heard at a distance of a mile or two.

Is more than one instrument necessary?

Both the speaker and hearer should be provided
with one, although by simply using the ear, or middle
funnel, a low whisper may be heard 1000 feet distant,
and walking through grass much farther,

What is the Tasimeter?

It is an instrument so constructed as to be very sensitive to the least degree of heat.

What use may be made of it?

It can be applied to many purposes; one of the most important being in the study of astronomy.

Will you explain in what way?

Telescopes being used for discovering stars, etc., not visible to the naked eye, the Tasimeter is attached to a large telescope, and the instrument directed to a part of the heavens where no heavenly bodies have been discovered.

What follows?

If there should be any star in this blank space, either non-luminous, or so far distant that it cannot be revealed by the telescope, it would be made known by the least variation in the Tasimeter.

When was this instrument successfully used?

At the last great eclipse, July 29th, 1878.

What is the latest invention of Mr. Edison.

The latest, and perhaps the most important, is the application of electricity to lighting private houses and public buildings.

Have any such attempts been made before?

Yes, very frequently; but none of them have been successful.

Who first produced electric light?

Faraday, a learned Englishman, in 1831, obtained a spark of electricity by motion; this may be considered as the origin of the ideas which have recently been utilized by Mr. Edison.

What advantage in his invention over previous attemps ?

Electric light has already been used, and although very powerful, it was too much concentrated upon one point. Mr. Edison removes this difficulty by making it radiate in all directions.

What peculiarity can you mention in this new invention ?

Although the light is very intense, yet *no heat whatever* is given out ; and as glass globes can be used with the burners, there will then be no danger of breaking them.

Is the light easily produced ?

It is more readily obtained even than gas.

Explain this.

No matches are required for lighting the burner ; it is only necessary to touch a spring, so that even a child can safely and easily use it.

Can you mention any other advantage ?

It can readily be introduced into any building, if gas is already in use there, as the same pipes can enclose the electric wire ; the patent burner of Mr. Edison may be placed at the end of the gas fixtures.

How is the degree of light regulated ?

This is done by springs.

Will the electric light be more expensive than gas ?

Mr. Edison says it will be much cheaper. Therefore, if this new invention proves a success, it may be regarded as one of the most important ever made.

SECTION XVI.

SUGAR.

CHAPTER I.

SUGAR.

How long has sugar been an article of trade?

This is not certainly known, but the ancient Jews are supposed to have used it. In the time of Alexander, 325 B.C., his admiral, Nearchus, found it among the people in the East Indies. The best sugar was produced in India.

When was it first brought to Europe?

It was carried there from Asia, in A.D. 625. The cultivation of the cane commenced in Sicily, being brought from Tripoli and Syria, then it passed to Madeira, afterwards to the West Indies and America.

When was it introduced into England?

Probably before the time of Henry VIII., though this is not certainly known.

Where is it raised in great quantities?

In Cuba and Louisiana. as well as in other places.

From what is sugar obtained?

From the sugar-cane, beets, and maple-trees.

What can you say of sugar-cane culture in the United States.

It was first introduced into Louisiana, in 1751, but made little progress for the next fifty years.

What change then took place?

The revolution of 1794, in St. Domingo, caused the French people, who lived there, to fly for their lives, with a few faithful slaves. They took refuge on board some American vessels, and as there were many French residents in Louisiana, they concluded to settle in that State. To these refugees we are indebted for the Creole cane, a small, yellow kind, then only cultivated in the French Islands.

By whom was sugar-cane introduced into Georgia?

By an enterprising farmer, who obtained 100 canes from the Otaheite Island. These soon increased to 2000, and from them nearly all the sugar plantations in Georgia and Louisiana have been formed.

How far did the culture extend?

It spread very rapidly to a distance of 150 miles from the sea, but the business on a large scale was soon after abandoned, enough only being raised for home consumption.

What was the cause of this?

The planters found that rice and cotton were more profitable in Florida and Georgia than the cane, and that Texas and Louisiana could produce more than double the quantity of sugar raised in the other States.

An acre in Texas yields 2400 pounds, while in Georgia, only 1000 pounds are produced from the same extent of land.

How many kinds of cane are cultivated in Louisiana ?

There are five species, viz. : *The Bourbon*, which has a dark purple color, and is very hardy. *The Green Ribbon*, being bright yellow, delicately striped with green. *The Red Ribbon* has narrow purple stripes, and is not affected by light frost.

What is the next variety ?

The Otaheite ; it has large joints, does not grow high, has a thin skin, and is not able to resist frost. The juice is very rich and abundant.

Describe the fifth species ?

This is called *The Creole Cane*, and produces a superior kind of sugar, but is not so much used as the Bourbon, being less hardy.

What can you say of the mode of culture ?

It is very simple, much like that of Indian Corn. The cuttings are planted in the Fall, usually in rows, three, five, and even sometimes eight feet apart, so as to be freely exposed to air and sun, during the nine months that are allowed for it to ripen. The cuttings are laid straight in the furrows that have been ploughed, and then covered with earth five or six inches deep.

How often is the cane planted ?

The time varies for different places. In Louisiana, usually once in three years ; further north, it must be

done annually ; but in the West Indies, and other tropical places, the cane will yield abundantly for 12, 15,
and even 24 years, from the same roots.

When is the cane gathered?

In Louisiana, the business usually begins in the
latter part of October, and must be done as quickly as
possible, to avoid frosts.

What is first done?

In this State, the seed does not ripen on the stalk,
therefore it is necessary to gather the part to be
planted again, and lay it on mats to be ripened in the
sun, being protected from frost by a mass of thick
tops, which cover it a foot deep.

What follows?

The crops are now cut off. For this purpose each
person has a large cane-knife, similar to a butcher's
cleaver. With the back of it he knocks off the dry
leaves, removes the unripe joints which cannot be
used, the rest of the stalk to the root is cut, and falls
to the ground. This part of the work is done very
rapidly.

Are the stalks left on the ground?

No ; they are gathered up by women and children,
taken in bundles to the wagons waiting to receive
them, and carried to the mill, which is usually built
eight or ten feet from the ground, that the juice may
flow into the boxes placed under them, when it is carried to the kettles for boiling.

Where are the canes placed in the mill?

They are spread evenly on the " *cane-carrier,*" which

is a belt revolving on a wheel, and carried by it to the heavy iron rollers. These press out the juice, which by boiling and evaporating changes it into muscovado.

What is Muscovado?

This is the name given to raw or unrefined sugar. It is placed in hogsheads with holes in the bottom, to allow the liquid part, called molasses, to flow through.

What is added to the juice while boiling?

A preparation of lime is used to purify the sugar, the juice being bleached by filtering it through "bone-black," that is, bones that have been changed to charcoal, by heating in a close vessel.

What is the capacity of the mills?

This varies in different places : some turn out 1000 gallons of juice per hour, for twenty hours each day, which produces 10 hogsheads of sugar, and 20 barrels of molasses.

How is the Muscovado sugar purified?

When properly boiled, it is poured into conical-shaped jars, with a hole in each. As soon as the molasses has drained off, the top is covered with some moistened clay. As this drains through the sugar, it carries off much of the impurities. This is then called "clayed," which can be refined by dissolving in water, and boiling again with some purifying substance, as blood, etc., when it is poured into the conical jars and covered with clay as before.

How is loaf sugar made?

This is the purest and best kind used. The raw

material is emptied into a pan having the bottom perforated with holes. Steam being applied to it below,
the sugar is dissolved. Some chemical substances
are added, that remove all color, leaving a pure white
article.

What follows.

It then passes to other pans, all the air is excluded,
and it is boiled by steam. As soon as it begins to
cool, the fine crystals or grains peculiar to loaf sugar
appear. When boiled enough, it is poured into
moulds in the loaf form, so that the sugar may remain
while the liquid passes off, the molasses being about
one-fifth of the whole quantity.

Is anything more necessary?

Sometimes a solution of lime is poured over the
loaf, and in passing through, any slight impurities that
remain are removed. The loaves are left to cool, then
packed in paper, marked, and ready for shipment.

*What can you say of the quantity of sugar used in
the United States?*

More is consumed here than in any European country, although not so much as in Cuba; enormous
quantities being used there for preserves, which are
very common as an article of food, besides much that
is exported. The people of this country are noted for
having a "*sweet tooth.*"

How much sugar is used for Candy?

Every year $8,000,000 are spent in making confec-
tionery.

What do you know of Stuart's refinery ?

It is one of the largest in the world. More than 300 men are employed ; and in one week 763 hogsheads, or 840,000 lbs. of sugar are used.

How does the machinery work there ?

The sugar is raised by steam power to the top of the building, emptied into an immense copper vat. Being soon dissolved by steam, while flowing through pipes and tanks, it is purified. At length it reaches the ground floor, where large barrels are ready to receive it, when it is shipped to various parts of the country.

How much is lost in refining ?

About 1½ lbs. of raw sugar will make one of white; and as much more of the refined sugar is in demand now than formerly, greater crops of the sugar-cane must be raised.

CHAPTER II.

MAPLE.—SORGHUM.—BEET SUGAR.

How is maple sugar obtained?

Maple trees being tapped, a sweet juice flows out, which is converted into sugar by boiling.

What is the color of it?

It is a dark brown. But by improvements in refining, the article can be made as pure and white as the finest loaf sugar.

How is this done?

It is boiled in a kettle, with potash, until a thick syrup is formed, which is strained when warm. After standing twenty-four hours, it is poured off, and can then be clarified.

Explain the process

For a quantity of 50 pounds a mixture of one quart of milk, an ounce of saleratus, the whites of two eggs well beaten, is boiled into the sugar until it becomes thick.

What follows.

This is drained through a tube, large at the top and coming to a point at the bottom. The sugar is put in when cold, the top covered with a thick, wet flannel, while the syrup and impurities drain through at the bottom, leaving the pure white sugar.

Where is the greatest quantity of maple sugar made?

Vermont and New York take the lead in the amount produced. Very little attention being given to the business in the Southern States. In 1860, about 39,000,000 pounds were made in the U. S., besides 2,000,000 gallons of maple molasses.

Has this amount been since increased?

Yes; in 1863, 1864 and 1865, the price of cane sugar advanced so much, that more attention was given to the making of the maple variety. In 1864, at least 30,000 tons were manufactured.

SORGHUM.

From what is Sorghum made?

The juice from the stalks of the Sorgho and Imphee, two plants of the maize family, when boiled, form a sweet syrup used as molasses.

Can sugar also be made from it?

Attempts have been made to produce this article, but with little success, as the syrup does not crystallize readily.

When was Sorghum first made?

The business commenced in 1850, gradually increasing, and during the late civil war advanced very rapidly on account of the high price of cane sugar and molasses.

How much was then produced ?

Probably not less than 50 or 60 millions of gallons. Since then it has declined, although still manufactured to some extent.

Has sugar been made from anything else ?

Very successful attempts have been made to produce it from the white sugar beet in California, Colorado, Wisconsin and Illinois.

How much has been made ?

In 1868 and 1869 not less than 300 tons, and now probably as many thousand are produced. The beet sugar is also extensively manufactured in France, Holland, and other parts of Europe. Sugar and molasses have also been made at Buffalo and a few other places from corn, by a chemical process.

SECTION XVII.

BEVERAGES

CHAPTER I.

TEA.

From what is Tea obtained?

It is the leafy product of a plant called " Thea," and belongs to the same family as the beautiful Camillas. The shrub is very bushy, growing to the height of from three to five feet, and sometimes even higher. It bears shining green leaves and white flowers, resembling the Myrtle.

Where is it found?

It is a native of China and Japan, also cultivated in and around India, and the Island of Java. The plant has been introduced into S. America, and, with the assistance of Chinese laborers, has been cultivated in Rio Janeiro.

Has it been raised in the United States?

An attempt was made in 1848, by Dr. Smith, to produce it in the mountainous part of S. Carolina.

For this purpose he imported plants of about five years' growth from China, and stocked a small planta-tion.

What success followed ?

Although exposed to severe frosts and snow, they were uninjured, and a fair crop was gathered, proving that our soil and climate are well adapted to the cul-ture of tea.

Has it since received much attention ?

It has not; as other crops can be raised with greater profit. Besides, it is difficult to find laborers who understand its cultivation. If it should become a staple of the country, California is probably the State where it will flourish most, as many Chinese live there, and the soil and climate are favorable to its growth.

Why is tea so expensive here?

Because it costs a great deal to transport it from the mountainous districts of China to the coast, then a long sea voyage follows before it reaches our shores, adding to the expense.

What is the cost of the article in China?

A fair quality of tea in the districts where it is raised, is valued at 8 or 9 cents per pound. The cost of packing, transportation, duties, etc., add only about 6 cents more, making the whole amount to but 15 cents before shipment to other countries.

How can it be raised so cheap?

This is owing to the low wages paid to laborers, generally only $3 or $4 per month, rates that could not be thought of in our country.

How long has tea been used as an article of drink ?

Various dates are given. The Japanese say that the Chinese first obtained it from Corea in the year 828, but this is not certain. It has not been traced back with certainty farther than the 9th century. Two Arabian travellers describe it as being then in use by the Chinese.

When was it first brought to Europe?

In the early part of the 16th century the Portuguese imported it. Travellers in China gave wonderful accounts of the virtues of tea in the 17th century, it being then generally used in Asia.

When was it used in England?

About 1650; and for many years was regarded as a rare and choice article at very grand entertainments. The Dutch East India Company imported much of it in the first part of the 17th century.

Did it soon become generally used ?

Not for some time ; as it was too expensive, except for the most wealthy persons.

What had been used before tea was introduced?

It was the custom in different parts of Europe to make hot drinks of various kinds of herbs, steeped in water ; the sage being one of the most common plants thus used. The Dutch are even said to have carried it to China to be exchanged for tea leaves.

What price was paid for tea ?

For some time after it was brought to Europe, from $30.00 to $50.00 per pound were the usual rates.

How was it sold?

It was retailed in the leaf form as we now buy it, and also as a liquid, being prepared to drink.

Did it soon become cheaper?

It must have continued very expensive for a long time ; as in 1664 a present of 2 pounds 2 ounces, valued at $25.00, was made to the King of England by the East India Company, and two years afterwards another similar present which was even more costly than the other.

How was the quantity of tea in Europe increased?

In 1677 the East India Company began to import it, but the duties were for a long time so heavy that it was regarded more as an article of luxury than of use.

What were some of the practices adopted by the traders?

They smuggled, or brought into the market without paying duties, great quantities of tea adulterated, and even sold a counterfeit for the real article.

What is the meaning of adulterated?

To adulterate any thing is to mix some poorer article with the pure ; in this way much money is made dishonestly.

Is this practice ever followed now?

It is ; not only in selling tea, but also coffee, sugar, and many other things : a fine is the penalty for such an act.

Are heavy duties now paid on tea in England?

Since 1834 they have been much diminished, so that

all classes of persons, rich and poor, can have this beverage.

How long has it been used in the United States?

To some extent the colonists always had it ; but it was not until 1790 that the tea trade became of much importance ; since then it has gradually increased

Is it in universal demand through the country?

We find it much more used in the north-eastern part, gradually diminishing towards the south, so that in some of the Southern States tea is almost and even entirely unknown. Coffee is substituted for it there, and to a great extent in the Western States.

Do the people of all nations prepare tea in the same way?

No ; we find different methods adopted. The most general is to steep the leaves in hot water.

What other method can you mention?

The Japanese always powder the leaf, and put it in porcelain cups filled with boiling water. The Persians boil the leaves until the water becomes black and acquires a bitter taste, when they add sugar, cloves, anise seed, fennel, etc.

What can you say of the Tartars?

They are very poor as a nation, and therefore use a common quality of the tea plant having coarse leaves. They press these with the stalks into little blocks, calling it " *Brick Tea.*"

How do they use it?

The Tartars lead a roving life, and on their long

journeys boil a lump of this tea, which makes the bad water they often find less disagreeable.

Is there more than one kind of tea ?

Yes ; we find many varieties, which either grow on different plants, or are prepared in various ways from the same bush.

CHAPTER II.

TEA (*Cultivating*).

Where do we find tea most extensively raised?

In a large portion of China, between 20° and 40° N. Latitude, extending east over the Japan islands, and west to Napaul and the Himalaya Mts. The most important part of this district in near the coast.

Are there any other countries where it is much cultivated?

In Japan, Tonquin and Cochin China, also in the mountainous parts of Ava, as well as in those places already mentioned.

On what kind of land is it raised?

The "garden tea," as it is called, is produced on the plains ; while that which grows on more elevated regions is named "hill tea," being far superior to the former.

Where is the best tea cultivated?

That in Napaul, on land nearly 5000 feet above the Bay of Bengal, is considered superior to any other. It brings from $1.50 to $1.75 per pound in the India markets.

Is very rich soil necessary ?

No ; for sometimes flourishing tea-fields may be seen on hill-sides, where no other green shrub appears.

When are the seeds planted ?

In the Spring ; having been buried in sand during the Winter. Some six or eight are sown in holes about four feet apart.

If the season should be dry, what is done ?

The young plants are moistened with rice water, or some other nutritious liquid, and if the winter is severe, are protected by straw wrapped around them.

When are the leaves gathered ?

Not until the second or third year. Sometimes the young leaf buds are picked early in April for the *Pekoe tea*, the best black variety known.

Do any other leaves appear ?

Yes ; these are gathered late in April and early in May, forming the most important part of the crop.

Are there any more ?

There is a third gathering early in July, and sometimes even a fourth in August and September, but the leaves are large, and the tea produced of an inferior quality.

How often are the plants renewed ?

They will usually bear for ten or twelve years, when the old ones are dug up, and give place to seedlings.

How are the leaves gathered ?

The laborers strip them off very rapidly into baskets of split bamboo, and being carried to a building they are sorted, and then dried.

Describe these buildings.

They seem to be low sheds, more or less open at the sides. Within are seen rows of pans in stacks of brick work, ready to receive the tea leaves.

Is the drying always done in the same way ?

The method varies with the different kinds of tea to be prepared. Sometimes the leaves are exposed to the sun in shallow pans, others are dried by being tossed up in the air.

How is a very choice variety dried?

That it may not be injured by handling, it is whirled around in sieves.

What follows ?

The leaves are then exposed to a gentle heat, sufficient to dry the moisture, but not enough to injure the aroma of the tea.

Is this done by machinery ?

No ; a person is required for each pan, to keep it constantly in motion with the hand. A brisk wood fire is kept under the pans during this operation.

What is then done ?

In a few minutes the leaves become soft, pliable, and moist upon the surface ; they are then thrown on a bamboo table, the workmen roll them in their hands, giving to the leaves the curled appearance common to imported tea.

Explain the next step in the process ?

The leaves are exposed to the air on a bamboo screen, then roasted with less heat over a charcoal; instead of a wood fire ; they are again rolled, these processes being sometimes once more repeated.

How are they finally dried ?

This is done—for the finest sorts—in pans over a very gentle charcoal fire.

What is the difference between green and black tea ?

The latter is exposed to the air for a longer time before the drying, as well as while it takes place. The leaves are sometimes spread for a whole night on bamboo mats, then tossed about and exposed to the air before being put in the pans. This causes the change of color from green to black.

In what other respect do they differ?

As the green is not exposed to the air for so long a time, the peculiar qualities of the plant are retained, as appears from the effect of the tea upon the nervous system.

Are both kinds of tea raised on the same land ?

Many assert that the plants furnishing black tea are raised on hilly places, while the green is obtained from the level lands that have been well fertilized.

For which kind is there a greater demand?

The green is more highly prized.

What have the Chinese done in consequence of this ?

They have colored inferior or damaged black teas, so as to make them pass for the higher priced green variety, and also improved the color of the poorer quality of the green to increase its value.

How is this done ?

An English nobleman, Sir John Davis, who witnessed the process, says that the Chinese first stir a little pulverized yellow turmeric among the leaves, while heated in the pans, and then add a mixture of gypsum and Prussian blue. Sometimes indigo and porcelain clay are also used.

Is this fraud still practiced ?

It is ; so that nearly, if not all, the green teas exported from China are colored or glazed.

What is also done to some black teas ?

Some kinds, as the " Orange Pekoe," " Black Gunpowder," or " Scented Caper," are made to appear smooth and glossy by rolling the leaves in pulverized black lead.

Are all kinds adulterated ?

Usually only the finer sorts ; the more common, as Souchong and Cougons, are free from these mixtures.

What other methods of deception are practiced by the Chinese ?

They often mix leaves of the ash, plum, etc., with the pure tea, and even go so far as to make a spurious article, having no real tea-leaves in it.

What name do they give it ?

They call it themselves the " Lie Tea " and even so mark the chests containing it.

How do they prepare it ?

The " Lie Tea " is made of the dust of tea and other leaves mixed with sand ; by adding a little starch or gum, these substances will unite in little masses, which are then colored to imitate either the black or green variety. The " Lie Tea" is also mixed with the pure article.

How is this known?

When steeped in boiling water the leaves will not unfold.

How are the different flavors given to tea?

The Chinese add the leaves of sweet-scented flow- ers, which are dried, powdered, and sprinkled over the tea-leaves, or else the leaves of each herb are arranged in layers, and all roasted together until the flowers be- come crisp, when they are removed by sifting.

What is the average product of a tea-farm?

Usually not more than 600 chests each, annually.

How are they sold?

The tea merchants purchase enough from each farm to make about 620 or 630 chests, which they mix to- gether, adulterate, roast again, then pack in chests for transportation, being sold to another merchant.

What does he do with them?

He puts upon them some mark, denoting the kind and quality of the article, and forwards them to the ship- ping ports.

How are they carried?

Through some of the districts the transportation is done by men, who place a bamboo stick across their shoulders, and put a chest on each end of it.

Is there any other method?

If the tea is of superior quality, greater care is taken. A single chest is fastened at the end of two bamboos and carried on the back of each man ; the other ends project in front, and are tied together. If he wishes to rest in going up the mountains, he places these two ends upon the ground, leaving the chest upright in the air, which relieves him of the weight.

Is there any other reason for this?

It is done so that the chest may never be defaced, or the tea injured by touching the ground. It is also shipped in boats as well as by porters.

How long does it take to perform these journeys?

From the Bohea districts to Canton, six to eight weeks, and to Shanghai, distance 620 miles, 28 days are required.

From what sea-ports in China are the principal exports made?

Chiefly from Shanghai, Foochow and Canton. The first and most northern of these places ship nearly all the tea used in the U. S. About twice as much is exported to Great Britain as to this country. The English generally prefer tea to coffee.

21

CHAPTER III.

COFFEE.

Was Coffee much used by the ancients ?

Probably not, as we find no traces of it among their ruins, or any account of it in their writings.

To what nation are we indebted for it?

Its use is traced to the Arabians, who are supposed to have obtained it from Abyssinia, where it has been in use for centuries. As good coffee is raised there as in Arabia. In 1454 it was much used in the latter country ; thence passed into Egypt and Syria. It grows wild in Siberia and Ethiopia.

When was it introduced into Europe ?

In 1511, in Constantinople, where coffee houses were opened about fifty years later. M. Thevenot first brought it to France in 1662—some 20 years before it was used in England.

In what countries is the coffee-plant raised ?

Besides those already mentioned, it is cultivated in Java, Brazil, Surinam and the West Indies.

Where is Surinam ?

It is a Dutch colony in S. America.

How was it introduced there?

In the year 1700, Gov. Van Horne, a Dutch gentleman, procured seeds from Mochá, and reared coffee-plants in Java; he sent one of these as a curiosity to the Botanical Garden at Amsterdam.

What resulted?

The seeds from this plant were sent by the Dutch to their colony at Surinam, and from these all the coffee of S. America has been produced.

Is it raised in the U. S.?

The heat of summer is not sufficient to ripen the seeds; while the cold of winter would kill the young plants. Nearly all we use is obtained from Brazil and St. Domingo—the former country furnishing nearly 8 per cent. of our supplies.

When does an English writer first mention the use of coffee.

In 1621, Burton, writing of the Turks, says: "They have a drink called coffee (for they use no wine), so named of a berry as black as soot, and as bitter, which they sip up warm as they can," etc.

How large is the coffee-plant?

Generally it is 8 or 10 feet in height, but when allowed to grow, will sometimes attain 30 feet.

What is the appearance of it?

The bark is of a gray color; the white flowers grow in clusters around the branches.

When cultivated, is it allowed to grow to its full height?

No; this is checked by cutting off the upper

branches, when the slender ones below spread out and bend over like those of an apple tree ; in this way the fruit is more easily gathered.

How are the plants raised?

They are produced first from seed in the nurseries, and when a year old are transplanted, being set out in rows. They are in full bearing in three years, and will thus continue for 20 years, and even longer.

What is then done with them?

As the shrubs and land are both exhausted, the owner abandons the old plantation, and forms a new one by cutting down a forest of trees and clearing the land.

Cannot the former Fazenda be cultivated by enriching the soil so as to be used again?

Certainly, it might ; but the people of S. America and most tropical countries seldom have forethought enough for that, although it is occasionally done.

When is the coffee gathered?

There are two principal seasons for harvesting, viz. : the late spring and fall, although at all times the ripe fruit may be gathered.

Why is this so?

The coffee plant being an evergreen shrub, the foliage is always fresh and seldom without some blossoms. The latter are continually appearing while the old flowers form into fruit.

Describe this fruit.

When ripe, it is red at first, then changes to a dark purple. It resembles a cherry, the fleshy part of which is very sweet and pleasant to eat. Two flat coffee beans form the seed of each one.

What is done with the fruit when ripe ?

In Arabia, where no heavy rains prevail that would beat it to the ground before being perfectly ripe, it is allowed to remain until just ready to fall, and then shaken on cloths spread under the bushes. The superior quality of the Arabian coffee is probably owing to this fact of its becoming so very ripe before gathering.

What is the process in other countries ?

The fruit is gathered by hand in the West Indies and S. America. At the harvesting season men, women and children may be seen scattered about the plantations, having broad shallow trays made of plaited grass or bamboo strapped over their shoulders, and supported at the waist.

How do they use them ?

They gather the coffee berries in these trays—some are a bright red, others beginning to dry, while a few are yet green, but will soon ripen in the hot sun.

What can the children do ?

They sit on the ground picking up the berries that fall under the bushes, singing gayly at their work.

What is then done with the fruit?

The custom at a South America fazenda, or coffee plantation, is for each one to carry his basket, when filled, to the superintendant, who empties it and gives in return a metal ticket, marked with the amount of work done.

What use is made of the ticket?

Each one is required to do a certain task each day; of course more for the men and less for the children. At night all present their tickets; those who have done more than the allotted work are paid for it at once.

After gathering the fruit what follows?

It must be dried : this is done on a level piece of ground usually at the foot of the coffee hills, the fruit being brought down in carts. Sometimes the roads are so bad that teams cannot travel there, and men are obliged to bring the harvest down the steep declivities on their heads.

How are the drying lots prepared?

The level ground is laid out in regular plats, paved with cement of dazzling whiteness. This forms a kind of square, around which are built low white houses for the use of the laborers. Adjoining this is a larger house occupied by the owner or overseer and family.

When ready for drying what is done with the fruit?

It is spread on the place prepared, several inches in thickness, and exposed to the heat of the sun ; when quite dry, the fruit is passed between a grooved roller and a board, so that the pulp may be washed off.

Is the process now ended?

Not quite ; a tough membrane still adheres to the seed—this is removed by a pair of heavy rollers, the chaff is winnowed out, when nothing but the coffee seeds remain.

Can they be used at once ?

Yes ; but age is said to improve them so much, that the very poorest coffee raised in America will in 10 or 12 years become equal to the very best produced in Turkey. The Arabian coffee usually requires only three years to obtain the same result.

What can you say of the raw coffee bean ?

It is very tough and horny, requiring to be roasted, so that it may be easily ground and dissolved in water.

What should be done with it after roasting ?

It must be closely covered in a box, that the aroma may be absorbed again ; otherwise it will evaporate, or pass into other substances, thus losing its strength and flavor.

Is this the case with raw coffee ?

It is to such an extent that it is not considered best to ship it in vessels previously freighted with sugar, etc. ; sometimes a few bags of pepper have spoiled a whole cargo of coffee.

Do all nations use coffee alike ?

No ; in Asia the natives make a thickened drink of it. In Sumatra the leaves are used instead of the seed ; the plant may be cultivated for the leaves in places where the soil and climate is not adapted to ripening the seed.

How are the coffee leaves used?

They are roasted a little, then rubbed to powder in the hands, when it is prepared for drink like tea, which it is said to resemble, as well as coffee, in taste.

Where do we find coffee mostly used?

In the warmer parts of the earth. In tropical countries it is the principal, even sometimes the only beverage, and although used very freely, no injurious effects appear.

Is it the same in cold countries?

No; it is used less frequently, being considered unhealthy. The preference is given to tea

Is coffee ever adulterated?

This is frequently and easily done by the addition of vegetable and other substances. Chicory is much used for this purpose.

How is it known?

By dissolving in cold water : if the liquid quickly turns brown, the coffee is adulterated ; but if it changes very slowly the article is pure, as coffee does not readily impart its color to cold water.

What is chicory?

It is a plant belonging to the same family as the dandelion, found growing wild in England and most parts of Europe.

Is it seen in this country?

The plant has been naturalized here, and is often found in the fields and along the road-sides. Its blossoms, of a bright blue color, appear in August and September

What use is made of it?

Formerly it was employed as a medicine, but of late has become a substitute for coffee, or used as an adulteration of it.

How is it prepared ?

The roots are dried and ground to powder, which resembles the color of ground coffee, but it has not the flavor or qualities of the article. The drink is, however, not unpleasant, and being very cheap the poor are glad to use it.

CHAPTER IV.

CHOCOLATE AND COCOA.

What is chocolate ?

It is a very nutritious drink prepared from cocoa, the fruit of a tree introduced into Europe from Mexico, in 1520, by the Spanish conquerors.

How did they regard it ?

It was considered very valuable as well as pleasant. They thought it so nutritious, that a single cup of it was considered sufficient to sustain a soldier through a day's march.

How is it prepared ?

The cocoa beans are roasted, ground very fine, made into a paste, and mixed with various articles to flavor and perfume them. This is done by rolling them in the paste while warm. It is then poured into moulds, when the chocolate comes out in the form of cakes, and is ready for market.

What are some of the substances added to the chocolate ?

The Aztecs, an ancient tribe of Mexicans, used vanilla and different spices; the French added musk and various perfumes. Other Europeans also used sugar, and, like tea and coffee, even adulterated it with wheat flour, sago meal, arrow-root, honey, molasses, etc.

How great was the adulteration?

It was carried to such an extent that a famous chemist found often that more than ½ of the chocolate sold in England was composed of these or similar substances.

Is the flavor improved thereby?

No; it is very inferior to the pure *chocolate;* this is probably one reason that it is not esteemed as highly as in the countries where the real article is sold. The object in adulterating it is to render the manufacture cheaper.

Is chocolate used for any other purpose?

A variety of sweetmeats are made from it.

Where is the cocoa tree found from which chocolate is made?

It abounds in the countries of Central and South America, and in the West India Islands, where it sometimes forms immense forests. It is also extensively cultivated in the Mauritius and Isle of Bourbon

What is the nature of the tree?

It is an evergreen, bearing fruit and flowers through the whole year, and growing to the height of 20 feet.

What can you say of the fruit?

It resembles a short thick cucumber, and contains 20 or 30 beans. These are arranged in five rows in a rose-colored pulp. Each one is about the size of a sweet almond, only thicker. The pulp, being similar to that of our watermelon, is used for food.

When is the fruit ripe ?

Usually it is ready to gather twice a year, in June and December, these being the principal crops ; although, like coffee, there is some ripe fruit at all times.

Where is the choicest kind obtained ?

The varieties from Central America are most highly esteemed.

How are the beans prepared for market ?

When the fruit is ripe the seeds are separated from the pulp and dried in the sun, when they are ready for sale.

Can you mention any other method ?

It is the custom in some countries to put the seeds in large tubs, when, being covered, they undergo a slight fermentation, by which they lose some of the sharp, bitter qualities peculiar to the fruit. They are stirred every morning while the fermentation is going on. The same object is attained in Mexico and other places, by burying the beans in pits dug in the earth.

What is then done with them ?

They are taken out and dried in the sun, when they are ready for market.

How are the dried beans used?

They can be roasted like coffee, after which they are turned out into shallow wooden vessels and stirred while cooling. Those that have fermented now split open into lobes like split beans, the shells falling off easily, which are about ⅛th of the whole weight.

Are the shells of any use?

Yes; they form an inferior quality of cocoa, called " *shells*," which is used as a drink.

What can be done with the split beans?

They may be used as food by long boiling; but for making chocolate they must be ground up and mixed with other substances, as already described.

COCOANUT.

Is the cocoanut obtained from the same tree as the cocoa?

No; it belongs to the natural family of palms, and is a native of nearly all tropical places, especially of islands and sand banks near the sea, and is often cultivated on extensive tracts of sandy soil; as along the coasts of Brazil, Ceylon, and the East Indies.

Will you describe the tree?

It has a straight trunk, without branches, growing to the height of 50 or 80 feet. The top is crowned with a cluster of feather-like leaves, 12 or 15 feet long.

Where do the flowers appear?

At the very top of the tree, where they grow in clusters—enclosed in a sheath. The nuts afterwards appear, 10 or 12 being usually bunched together

When does the tree begin to bear fruit?

Usually in the sixth or seventh year. It blossoms about once in six weeks during the rainy season, and produces each year 100 nuts.

Is the cocoa-nut tree of any other use?

Yes; many things are manufactured from different

parts of it. In fact, there is no tree in the world from which so many useful things can be made.

Will you mention some of them?

The natives thatch their houses with the leaves, and so durable is this covering, that for many years it serves as a protection from wind and rain. The finer fibres furnish material for a beautiful matting much used in the East Indies, while the coarser part is used for brooms and baskets.

Can you give any others?

The ashes make potash. The thick wood in the centre of the tree is used for oars; the thinner part being made into a kind of paper.

Is the sap of any use?

Yes; this is obtained by making incisions in the flower buds at the top of the tree, and daily collected by persons who climb up there for them. At first it resembles water in appearance, and is sold as a cooling drink in the markets.

What change does it undergo?

In a few hours it begins to ferment, when it has a sharp taste and intoxicates, like whisky. It is then called "palm-wine." When this is distilled, a very strong kind of ardent spirits is obtained, known to Europeans as "Arrack."

What else is obtained from the sap?

A poor quality of sugar; which, being boiled with quick lime, makes an excellent cement.

What does the nut contain?

A hard white substance, much used by the natives

as an article of food; also esteemed by foreigners. The white liquid called *milk* is an agreeable beverage. A valuable oil is also extracted from it, which is used for burning and other purposes.

What is done with the shell?

Drinking cups are made from it. The outer husks furnish an excellent fibre from which Indian cordage is made, being thought more durable than any other. Large quantities of it are exported every year from Ceylon and India to England.

When the cocoa-nut is half formed, what does it contain?

The white, hard part is then only a pulpy, cream-like substance, which is considered very delicious. It is eaten with a spoon; sugar and orange blossoms are added to flavor it.

How can you tell the age of the tree?

It produces leaves and fruit long before it attains its full height, so that the head is constantly pushing up from the trunk; and wherever the leaves have grown, two rings are formed around the tree, so that one year is allowed for every two rings. If there were 30 rings the tree would be fifteen years old.

Will you now give all the useful articles made from the cocoa-nut tree?

Bread, water, wine, vinegar, brandy, milk, oil, honey, sugar, needles, thread, cups, spoons, basins, baskets, paper, masts for ships, sails, cordage, nails, and covering for houses.

SECTION XVIII.

COAL.

CHAPTER I.

COAL.

What is coal?

This substance, so familiar to all, is composed of vegetable matter which has undergone a change while buried in the earth.

Will you describe its formation?

In the history of the world, there is supposed to have been a period, before the creation of man, when the earth was covered with gigantic vegetation, different from any known to us.

What caused it to grow thus?

At that time there was a great deal of carbon in the air, much more than we have now, and as this gas is the food of vegetable matter, all plants and trees then grew to a wondrous size.

How was the wisdom of God thus shown?

As animals can live on but little carbon, requiring

more oxygen for their support, they could not have existed at that time ; the vegetation, therefore, then took up the carbon, leaving the air pure, and fit for men and animals.

Were there any animals at that time ?

Some of the lower orders are supposed to have existed, as remains of shell-fish, corals, fishes, and a few reptiles, have been found in the coal regions.

Was the vegetation forming the coal all buried at the same time ?

This must have been done at different periods ; as separate beds of coal are found with layers of earth between them.

In what position are the formations ?

The fossil forests composing coal beds are often found erect, the change having taken place while the trees and plants were still standing. Sometimes, also, these immense forests are found piled one above another.

Can you give any instance of this ?

Near Cape Breton at least 59 distinct forests have been traced out, one above the other. Also off the Bay of Fundy are high cliffs, where may be seen 17 tiers of fossil forests, measuring 4500 feet from base to summit.

What do we infer from this ?

It is probable that above the lowest tier earthy matter gradually accumulated, forming a foundation for the next forest, which, by the aid of carbon, soon arrived at its full growth, and in its turn became the

22

basis of another series of vegetation, thus continuing through the whole strata.

Are different forms of the material composing coal ever seen ?

Yes; frequently in the mines may be discovered the delicate foliage, with scaly stems and drooping branches, as perfectly preserved as when first formed.

What may be seen in the mines of Bohemia ?

In the different galleries of these mines, the extinct foliage is found in great profusion, hanging from the arched roof and walls, so delicate and beautiful that the most elaborate works of art can give no idea of its grace and elegance.

Did the vegetation of the coal period resemble that of the present day ?

Very little, if at all ; being composed of reeds, pines, palms, etc., differing in size and appearance from those we now see.

Has coal always been used for fuel by man ?

Probably not ; although some writers say that the ancient Britons must have burned it instead of wood, as it is found in such abundance in England.

When are we certain that it was discovered ?

About 1230, at New Castle-upon-Tyne, we first hear of coal being used. But it was not until 50 years later that it became an article of trade between that place and London.

How was it regarded at first ?

It was generally considered so injurious to the health that it was regarded as a public nuisance, and does not seem to have been commonly used in London until 1400, or throughout England until the time of Charles II., 1625.

Is coal used for any thing except fuel?

Yes ; a kind of luminous gas is obtained from it, besides various substances useful in the arts.

How many kinds of coal can you mention?

There are four principal varieties, viz.: anthracite, bituminous, cannel and brown.

What is the anthracite coal?

It is a very hard, pure variety, from which the bitumen has been expelled; that which is left being mostly carbon. The word anthracite is from the Greek, and means "consisting of carbon." It burns without smoke or smell.

Where is it found?

In many parts of England, and very extensively in the eastern portion of the United States. This kind of coal was once bituminous, but being purified from its volatile gases assumed its present form.

What is the extent of the anthracite coal bed in the Middle States?

In Pennsylvania, where it is found in greatest abundance, the formation covers an area of over 30 miles, being many feet in thickness. Detached beds also appear in many places near the main locality, so that it is supposed to underlay about one-third of the State.

What can you say of the bituminous coal?

This is an inferior quality, found in the Western

States more than at the East, and is so called from the quantity of bitumen found in it.

What is bitumen?

It is a kind of inflammable substance found in the earth, something of the nature of pitch, giving out a strong odor while burning.

Are there any varieties of this substance?

Yes; and different names are given, which indicate its gradual change from a vegetable to a mineral state, as lignite, bituminous wood, bituminous coal, etc.

What may sometimes be seen in the same bed?

These different varieties are often found together, so that the changes through which the wood passes before becoming a mineral may be readily traced out.

What is cannel coal?

This variety is very hard and brittle, and takes a fine polish, so that ink-stands, snuff boxes, etc., are sometimes made of it.

Why is it so called?

The word cannel is a corruption of *candle*, as pieces of this coal are sometimes used in England and Ireland instead of lamps or candles.

How does brown coal differ from those already mentioned?

It is only partially converted into the mineral state, being generally found in beds near the surface of the earth.

Is coal always seen below the level of the sea?

No; it is sometimes discovered at great elevations.

One writer states that it has been found on the Cordilleras, in S. America, 13000 feet above the sea level.

What is sometimes found with mineral coal ?

Charcoal is often mixed with it ; and occasionally a piece will be seen; one side of which is charcoal, while the other has become mineralized.

CHAPTER II.

USEFUL SUBSTANCES OBTAINED FROM COAL.

When coal is perfectly purified from all other gases except carbon what do we have ?

The diamond, which is pure carbon crystallized, that is formed into a solid with a certain number of smooth sides called *faces*.

How is coal usually found ?

In layers called beds, separated by slate, quartz, or some other kind of rock ; they are several miles in extent, and thousands of feet deep.

What is the size of the coal-fields in England ?

Those of Durham and Northumberland are 732 square miles in extent. The beds of Yorkshire are said to be inexhaustible. The coal in South Wales alone is so abundant, that it will supply all England for at least 2000 years.

Are there any others in Great Britain ?

Rich mines have been opened in Scotland and Ireland.

Is there any danger attending the working of mines ?

Frequent accidents happen to the workmen from

the machinery, falling of coal, and the explosions which took place.

What was the cause of the latter?

This was owing to a kind of gas, called "*fire-damp*," which formed in the mine, and when this came in contact with a lighted torch or candle, an explosion followed.

How are accidents of this kind now prevented?

Sir Humphrey Davy, a learned Englishman, invented a safety lamp in 1816, which can be carried through any part of a coal mine, and even plunged into this explosive gas without the slightest danger.

How was it made?

The cup or vessel for holding the oil has a spout at the side by which it is filled. On the top is placed a wire gauze cylinder, supported by three iron rods; this is closed by a cover, having a handle for carrying the lamp.

Was this invention the result of accident?

By no means; Mr. Davy made many experiments before accomplishing the work.

On what principle was this safety-lamp made?

The inventor found that although the gauze might be heated to white heat, yet that was not sufficient to make the gas explode; but the heat of flame being greater would cause such an explosion. The flame coming in contact with the wire cooled enough to prevent any explosion, as metals are excellent conductors of heat.

Can you give an experiment to illustrate this?

If a piece of wire gauze is placed over the flame of

a lamp, the hand can be held above it very close to the fire; but on removing the gauze the heat cannot be borne for an instant.

How can this gas be perceived in the mine?

It is known to be present by the loud explosions frequently heard: its power is very great. Frequently when a coal bed is first opened, the water enclosed will rush out with great violence; and as the miner strikes the rock with his pick, the gas explodes as if a pistol had been shot.

What does it even do to the coal itself?

It will burst pieces off the solid wall. If a river flows over the line where this gas forms, the water will be greatly agitated, and the vapor rising to the surface can be inflamed. When collected in cavities dug in the river bank, if ignited it will burn for months, unless extinguished.

In the burning of coal what may be obtained?

By distilling or burning in closed vessels, very use-ful products are obtained, as coke, coal-gas, coal-tar, naphtha, naphthaline, paraffine, benzole, coal-oil, etc.

From which kind of coal are these most readily pro-duced?

As the bituminous coal contains a greater variety of materials, more of these useful articles are obtained from it than from the purer anthracite.

What is coke?

It is the mineral coal from which the bitumen, sul-phur, etc., have been removed. This is done by burn-ing the coal in closed ovens, a hole being left in the top for the gas to escape : other methods are some-times adopted.

What use is made of coke ?

It is used in glass furnaces, on railroads, etc., where great heat is required. Experiments have proved that its heating power is ¼ greater than that of common coal.

Is coke ever found in a natural state?

Yes ; beds of it have been discovered on both sides of the James River, and at Richmond, Va., which are very productive.

What use is made of coal-tar?

This is obtained in making gas for burning, and at first was considered useless. Now, however, it is employed to cover machinery, as a protection from the weather, and when distilled, the pitch obtained being mixed with earthy substances, is used for pavements and water-proof covering of roofs.

If purified, what else is formed of coal-tar

Some oily fluids and naphtha.

What is naphtha ?

It is a kind of mineral oil, burning with a blue flame, having a strong odor of bitumen, and so inflammable that it takes fire even on the appearance of flame.

Is it found in a native state ?

Copious springs of naphtha are seen on the Caspian Sea. The earth in that region constantly sending up vapor from it. This substance is also seen in Siberia, Hungary, Sicily, etc.

What use is made of it ?

The streets of Genoa, Italy, are said to have been lighted with it. The people around the Caspian Sea collect the vapor in tubes, thus having perpetual light ; they also cook their food by this kind of fire.

Can you mention any other uses to which it is applied ?

When purified, it will readily dissolve caoutchouc, and mixed with wood-naphtha will make a solution of resinous substances, useful in various kinds of varnish.

When naphtha is still further purified what is obtained from it ?

A liquid called benzole, or benzoin, which is much used by India-rubber manufacturers, as it more easily dissolves the raw article than any thing else. It will be found very valuable for illuminating purposes when properly prepared.

What is carbolic acid ?

This is distilled from coal-tar, resembling creosote in taste and smell, and found very useful in the preparation of a valuable dye-stuff. Within a few years it has been extensively employed by physicians and surgeons. For the healing of wounds nothing has been found so quick and effective.

Can you mention any thing else obtained from coaltar ?

A heavier kind of oil than the last one mentioned may be formed, which, united with bleaching powder and other substances, makes a magnificent blue color that will probably be substituted for indigo in dyeing.

What is paraffine?

This is also another valuable oily substance produced from coal-tar, entering largely into the manufacture of candles. If the tar is distilled at a higher temperature a solid white substance is obtained, called naphthaline.

What use is made of it?

It yields two coloring substances, one of which seems to be of the nature of madder, for when mixed with certain alkalies, a beautiful red color is the result.

What can you say of the value of coal-tar?

That which at first was regarded as worthless proves to be almost invaluable.

What other very useful article is obtained from coal mines?

Petroleum, or coal-oil. In opening a new section of a mine, on striking the rock a quantity of this fluid will gush out, as water from a well. Those places are therefore called oil wells.

Where are they found?

Generally in places near coal formations ; more abundantly in some localities than others. Asia seems to furnish it most plentifully.

What is found in the Burman Empire?

In one neighborhood there are 520 wells in full activity, into which the petroleum flows from coal formations, producing more than 400,000 hogsheads annually.

What use is made of it?

It is burned in lamps instead of other oil, and when mixed with earth or ashes is used for fuel.

Is coal-oil found in this country?

Within the past twenty years several wells have been struck in Pennsylvania, proving a source of immense wealth to the owners, taking the place of both sperm and whale-oils, so that not half as much of the latter is now sold as formerly.

What advantage in the use of it?

Coal-oil is found much cheaper, besides burning with a brighter, clearer light than whale-oil. The chief objection to its use is the danger of explosion when coming in contact with flame. Serious accidents have often occurred in this way.

CHAPTER III.

GAS.

What is gas ?

This term is applied to any elastic fluid which will neither become solid or liquid at ordinary temperatures.

To what form of gas do we now refer ?

To that which is used for illuminating purposes.

How is it obtained ?

By distilling coal in a retort or closed vessel.

Is it ever found in a natural state ?

Yes ; since the earliest ages, in various countries, it has issued from crevices in the earth, probably caused by the decay of different substances.

How much can be obtained at these places ?

The supply seems inexhaustible, as it has come from the same localities for centuries.

Is it always in the coal region ?

No ; frequently it is below that formation. The most celebrated natural fountains of this kind are on the borders of the Caspian Sea.

Is it found in the United States?

In the Western part of New York these fountains come from the slate and sandstone region, so pure and abundant as to be collected in gasometers, and carried through pipes for lighting the neighboring villages.

Mention some places where natural gas is thus used?

The town of Fredonia, N. Y., has been illuminated in this way for many years; also the light-house at Portland, Lake Erie.

What have the Chinese done?

For a long time they have used jets of gas obtained from their salt wells, both for fuel and for lighting their streets and houses, by evaporating the brine.

Is the light from natural gas as brilliant as that from the artificial?

Its illuminating power is less, owing to the want of an equal amount of carbon.

How long has the artificial gas been known?

Its discovery is due to Dr. Clayton, an Englishman. The account of his experiments appear in a letter dated May 12, 1688.

How was it done?

Having distilled some coal in a retort, he accidentally noticed that the gas issuing forth was inflammable. He collected this in bladders, and amused his friends by lighting it, as it came from the holes pricked in the bags.

Were these experiments made practically useful?

Although many persons besides Dr. Clayton distilled this gas from coal, the object for some time seemed only to exhibit something curious and wonderful.

When was it first used for lighting houses?

In 1792 Mr. Murdoch, an Englishman, made experiments for this purpose, and five or six years later fitted up an apparatus for lighting a manufactory with which he was connected.

What progress did he make in the business?

In 1804–5 he prepared the largest machinery yet constructed, which furnished light for some mills at Manchester equal to nearly 3000 candles. In 1814, the streets of London, near Westminster Bridge, were thus lighted for the first time.

Of what other material was gas made?

It was produced from refuse oily and fatty substances, the gas being of a superior quality.

Did the business prosper?

It was at length abandoned, as the cost of the raw material was found to be greater than coal.

Has any such attempt been made in the United States?

Within a few years it has been successfully carried on; cheap rosin oil being used for the purpose.

How is it made?

The rosin oil is dropped upon a heated metal surface, the gas at once appears, and can be conducted immediately into the gasometer without further purification. Rosin itself has also been applied to the same purpose.

From what other material has gas been obtained ?

For some time it has been made from wood, and used in Philadelphia. In Germany, this kind of gas was also employed for lighting towns.

How is it prepared ?

The wood, being thoroughly dried, is placed in red-hot retorts. The gas is immediately given off and passes into the apparatus for purifying, then distributed by pipes to the places required.

What is obtained besides gas ?

A quantity of useful tar ; besides this, the charcoal that remains in the retort, which is more valuable even than the coke obtained from coal.

Is gas made from anything else ?

Water has been used for this purpose, and benzole more successfully ; also peat.

What experiment was made at Rheims ?

The soap water left after washing woollen stuffs has been found to contain much oily matter. By adding sulphuric acid, the greasy part rises to the surface : this is collected and distilled, when the gas is given off very freely

In making gas from coal, what variety is preferred?

The cannel is considered the best for this purpose, as giving out a greater quantity and better quality of the article required.

Where is it obtained?

It is exported from England to this country. Some of the mines in Virginia and the Western States also furnish it.

What is necessary in forming the coal into gas?

The retorts, which are of clay or cast-iron, are heated to redness as quickly as possible, and kept at this temperature.

Why is it necessary?

At a lower heat it is found that much tar and other substances are formed, of less value than the gas. The coal should also be as dry as possible, for if it contains much moisture, the steam given off will cool the retort.

What length of time is required to form the gas?

This varies with the size of the retort and the kind of coal used. Generally from four to six hours are required. In Scotland, however, the rich cannel coal found there will yield gas in three hours.

What is the amount obtained?

This also depends upon the quality of coal. The average yield is about 1000 cubic feet to a ton, or one-tenth of the material used.

How is the value of the gas estimated?

By comparing it with the light of a certain number of candles.

Will you give an instance?

An ordinary burner will consume about five cubic feet of gas in an hour. The gas of the London works is equal to the light of from 12 to 18 candles : that of Liverpool is far superior, sometimes equal to 22 candles. In New York it seldom reaches 20 candles, the average being about 16.

In manufacturing gas, what is the most necessary part of the work ?

The retorts require first attention. These are immense iron or clay cylinders, set in brick fire-places, and contain the coal to be formed into gas.

How many are used at once ?

The number varies from three to thirteen in each furnace. They are usually set in horizontal rows, with a fire under each of the lower retorts, so that the flame can pass among them all before reaching the flue

In large establishments, what are seen ?

The furnaces extending through the length of a large building, with many hundred retorts, all in operation through the winter, but only a part in summer.

When the retorts are filled with coal, what is then done ?

Before lighting the fire, they are made air-tight by means of a door at the outer end, which is closely cemented.

As the gas forms, what becomes of it ?

It passes through iron pipes into a large tube, called the " Hydraulic Main," half filled with water, which takes the impurities from the gas.

What is then done ?

Any impurities that still remain are removed by the "lime purifier," a mixture of lime and water, or lime alone, through which the gas passes ; the latter is generally preferred.

How is it known to be of good quality ?

During the process it is frequently tested by hold

ing a piece of paper, wet with a solution of sugar of
lead, to a jet of the gas. If it is discolored at all the
gas is impure.

After purifying the gas, what is then done?

It is conducted to the " station meter," an instru
ment that measures and registers the quantity produced, on the same principle as the meters used by
the consumers at each house, although, of course, on a
much larger scale.

Will you describe it?

A circular box, more than half full of water, contains
a drum, supported on a rod passing from end to end
of the outer case. This drum is divided into four
equal parts, opening into the space around the axis.
By means of slits in the rim, it also communicates
with the outer part.

How does the drum work?

The gas being admitted into the central space, flows
into one of the divisions of the drum which is partly
under water. As this gradually fills, the pressure of
the gas causes the drum to revolve, bringing the next
division into a position to be filled, and so on.

As each chamber is filled, what becomes of the gas?

By turning the drum, it is emptied into the space
above the water next to the outer case, being con-
veyed from there to the gas-holder.

How is the quantity of gas indicated?

The amount that each chamber will hold is already
known ; the number of revolutions made by the drum
is recorded by wheel-work connected with dials on the

outside of the box, by which the whole quantity of gas passed through is readily seen.

What is the next apparatus ?

It is the gasometer or gas-holder. This is made of sheet-iron, painted, being open at the bottom, and set in a tank of water.

Explain its action.

On admitting the gas below, the cylinder is raised up. When any is required, a stop-cock being turned, the pressure of the gasometer forces the gas through pipes laid for its passage.

What is the size of the gasometer?

It varies in proportion to the amount of gas required. One in Philadelphia will hold more than 1,000,000 cubic feet of gas at a time, being 70 feet high and 140 in diameter. That in London is one-third larger.

How long has gas been used in this country ?

The first attempts to introduce it were made at Baltimore, more than 50 years ago, but without much success. In 1822 it was introduced into Boston. The next year a gas company was formed in New York, but was not in successful operation until four years later.

What progress has since been made ?

The use of gas continued to spread with great rapidity, until all our principal towns and cities are now lighted with it.

In recalling what has been learned from this book, state the conclusions we may draw ?

We find the greatest improvements and most wonderful inventions are the result of American skill, industry and genius, and that these very discoveries in science and art will only prepare the way for still greater progress in the future.

What are the principal inventions of Americans now in use throughout the world?

1. The cotton gin, without which the machine-spinner and the power loom would be useless. 2. The plaining machine. 3. The grass mower and grain reaper. 4. The rotary printing press. 5. Navigation by steam. 6. The hot air, or caloric engine. 7. The sewing machine.

Can you mention any more?

8. The manufacture of India-rubber and gutta-percha goods. 9. The sand blast, for carving. 10. The grain elevator. 11. The electro-magnet and its practical application. 12. The most successful composing machine for printers. Other inventions might also be mentioned.

THE END..

Lightning Source UK Ltd.
Milton Keynes UK
UKOW06f2059200617
303778UK00012B/645/P